SUICIDE TERRORISM
RELEVANCE IN THE INDIAN CONTEXT

Lt Col Behram A Sahukar (Retd)

Established 1870

Published in association with
United Service Institution of India
New Delhi

Vij Books

Vij Books
Ansari Road, Daryaganj, New Delhi

Published by

Vij Books
(Publishers, Distributors & Importers)
4675-A, 21 Ansari Road
New Delhi - 110002
Phones: 91-11-65449971, 91-11- 43596460
Fax: 91-11-30126465
web : www.vanishbooks.com
e-mail : vijbooks@rediffmail.com

Views expressed in the monograph are of the author and not of the Institution.

The Monograph is a result of research allotted to Lt Col Behram A Sahukar (Retd) by the USI.

ISBN: 978-93-80177-08-3

Contents

CHAPTER 1

INTRODUCTION AND OVERVIEW

Introduction

Suicide Terrorism fuelled by religious extremism/nationalism poses one of the gravest threats to international security and stability today and has wide-spread ramifications throughout the world.[1] As is now well known, the ongoing United States (US)-led 'Global War on Terror' was triggered by mass casualty suicide attacks against the American mainland on September 11, 2001 by Islamists backed by Al Qaeda. The spate of suicide bombings by Palestinian resistance groups against Israeli occupation is the main cause of the multi-pronged harsh Israeli responses and continuing instability in the region. Suicide terrorism attacks by Islamic extremists have been devastatingly effective against coalition forces and civilian targets in the current Iraq war and against NATO-led coalition forces in Afghanistan. The July 7, 2005 London train suicide bombings by British-born Muslims led to unprecedented and widespread anti–Muslim sentiment throughout Europe, and to far reaching anti-terrorism legislation in Britain. Suicide terrorism against India such as the December 2001 Parliament attack by Pakistan-based Islamist terrorists compelled India to deploy for war against Pakistan, and plunged the region to the brink of a nuclear holocaust.[2] The spread of militant Islamist extremism and in particular the alarming increase in the number of suicide bombings within Pakistan was one of the main reasons given for the imposition of the Emergency by General Musharraf on November 3, 2007.[3]

Though an ancient and mediaeval tactic[4], the first major contemporary suicide terrorism attack was the December 1981 bombing of the Iraqi Embassy in Beirut (during the Iran-Iraq War probably by Iranian agents) that left 27 dead and over 100 persons wounded.[5] The use of suicide terrorism was subsequently developed into an effective strategic weapon in 1983 in Lebanon by the Iran-backed Shiite group the *Hezbollah*. *Hezbollah* was raised primarily to resist the 1982 Israeli invasion, and force the withdrawal of the Multinational Force (US, France, Italy and UK) that was deployed in Lebanon.[6] Until recently, the Liberation Tigers of Tamil Eelam (LTTE) had executed the most number of suicide terrorist attacks (over 240) worldwide. However, the rising number of suicide attacks in Iraq by Al Qaeda-inspired Islamist groups and Sunni-Shia rivals has far surpassed the total number of such attacks by Hezbollah, LTTE and all other terrorist groups combined. For example, Mohammed Hafez estimates that approximately 514 suicide terrorism attacks took place in Iraq alone from March 2003 to August 18, 2006.[7] Another estimate calculates the total number of suicide bombings in Iraq during the period March 2003-2008 as high as 1121.[8] In Afghanistan too, the Al Qaeda-inspired resurgent Taliban has conducted several suicide bombings against Afghan and US security forces and the NATO-led International Security Assistance Force (ISAF). Suicide attacks in Afghanistan are increasing daily with mounting casualties as the Islamist insurgency rapidly gains momentum.[9]

The recent spread of suicide terrorism has become a serious threat that confronts all countries from North America to South East Asia spanning a new 'Crescent of Crisis' that includes the Indian Subcontinent. Suicide terrorism has been practiced in the past by secular and religiously-motivated extremist groups alike.[10]

The data recorded by the RAND-Memorial Institute on Prevention of Terrorism (MITP) Terrorism Incident Database, National Counter Terrorism Center, and the South Asia Terrorism Portal at the Institute of Conflict Management all point to the disturbing fact that the number of suicide terrorism attacks and the resultant casualties is increasing daily with increasing casualties.[11] Though suicide terrorism attacks in India have steadily reduced in recent years, the July 2008 suicide bombing of the Indian Embassy in Kabul by radical Islamists of the Taliban is a reminder of the continuing threat of suicide attacks against Indian targets at home and abroad.[12]

Suicide Terrorism-Explained Briefly

What is suicide terrorism? The word 'terror' comes from the Latin root "*terrere*" which means 'to frighten' or to 'create intense or overpowering fear' (through violence or threat of violence). "Suicide" is a voluntary act to take one's own life i.e. 'to kill ones owns self' (from Latin *sui* 'of oneself'+ *cide* 'to kill'). Therefore, 'suicide terrorism' roughly means 'creating or instilling intense fear by willingly and violently taking one's own life (killing others while killing oneself).' President Bush has used the term 'homicide bombings' and some others refer to suicide bombings as 'murder by suicide'. Militant Islamists prefer the term "self-martyrdom/martyrdom operations" or "sacrificial explosions".[13] Boaz Ganor the Israeli counter terrorism expert has defined suicide terrorism as "a terrorist/operational act where the certain death of the attacker(s) is a pre-requisite for success of the operation".[14]

I have expanded this narrow definition to include that 'the *planned* certain death of the attacker is a pre-requisite for success.' Therefore, if the attacker engineers his own death during the operation by staying and fighting until he is killed by security forces during the attack; it would qualify as a suicide attack/an act of suicide terrorism.[15] In my view, the planned intention not to return alive and the genuine eagerness of the attacker to die in the terrorist attack is as good as 'killing oneself to kill others'.[16] It must be noted that despite lengthy debates on the subject, a universally acceptable definition of terrorism or suicide terrorism has not been agreed to by the international community.

Some Advantages of Suicide Terrorism

Suicide terrorism sometimes results in limited physical damage (except for the instantaneous death of the bomber), but the very act of self-detonation that defies the normal instinct of staying alive is itself one of psychological warfare that instils fear in the audience and attracts world-wide media attention. A sudden explosion in a public place such as a restaurant or on a bus by a person who a little while ago was perhaps sitting very calmly (and perhaps smiling) on the next seat, instils fear and suspicion in the targeted population. A simple bus journey or going out to get a cup of coffee could result in a fiery death or serious injury by a suicide bomber's 'sacrificial explosion'. Children on school buses, teenagers in a discotheque, commuters on a train, and normal people going about their daily routine to work or for recreation are all legitimate and lucrative targets for the predatory suicide bomber.

Ami Pedahzur of Haifa University and his team have assessed that suicide terrorism on an average tends to be more lethal than other forms of terrorism. While the average number of victims in a shooting attack is 3.32, and casualties in a remote-controlled explosive attack is 6.92, the average number of victims harmed by a suicide bomber wearing an explosive belt can be as high as 81.48 during one attack. When the suicide bomber is driving an explosive-laden car, the number of victims rises to an average of 97.81.[17] In Israel alone, more than 48 percent of the casualties caused by terrorism from 2000-2005 were due to suicide terrorism, though suicide terrorism itself amounted to less than one percent of all terrorist attacks.[18]

The suicide bomber is usually able to get very close to the target and is usually able to set off his explosives at will for maximum damage and effect. He is also able to avoid detection and can travel easily to attack an alternative target depending if the need arises because of heightened security conditions. The human suicide bomber has the flexibility to adapt to changing circumstances for maximum destructive and psychological effect before self-detonation and is sometimes referred to as the 'ultimate smart bomb'.

Additionally, there is no need for the suicide attacker to plan for an escape after the attack, nor does he/she fear capture or death, as his/her own death is part of the success plan of the suicide attack.[19] Suicide bombers have walked in calmly and purposefully or rammed their explosive laden vehicles and blown themselves up in banks, cafes, restaurants, hotel lobbies, market places, mosques, marriage parties, funerals, cinema halls, synagogues, churches, internet cafes, radio stations, railways stations, recruiting offices, police stations, at check points, in night clubs, against moving convoys and in hospitals. They have killed themselves in buses, trains, aircraft, trucks, boats, cars and on bicycles. It seems they never run out of new methods and new ideas of killing themselves and others for the cause they believe in so strongly. And they never seem to lack courage to detonate their body or have any pity for their innocent intended victims.

Spread of Suicide Terrorism

As mentioned above, the horrific success of the 9/11 suicide attack has given a fresh impetus to suicide attacks the world over.[20] Some of the other factors that have led to an increase in suicide terrorism (mainly by militant Islamists) are the prolonged US-led war in Iraq (2003), the ongoing Global War on Terror (and the resultant ascendancy of Islamist extremism), the resurgence of the Taliban in Afghanistan, Western counter terrorism policies and the prolonged deployment of Western-backed foreign military forces in the Middle East (West Asia) and the Muslim world (leading to a perception of anti-Muslim hostile intentions), and the unresolved Israeli-Palestinian Conflict (US support for Israel and its harsh policies against the Palestinians). In addition, Islamist suicide bombers have also attacked targets in moderate Muslim/secular countries (US allies in the war against terror) such as Jordan, Saudi Arabia, Turkey, Yemen, Morocco, Algeria, Pakistan, Tunisia, Philippines, and Indonesia for their support to Western policies considered to be anti-Muslim and contrary to the Islamists' interpretation of 'true' Islamic tenets and principles.[21]

Suicide terrorism has spurred a lot of recent academic research. Many books have been published recently on this subject in quick succession.[22] Robert Pape of the University of Chicago and the widely acclaimed author of 'Dying to Win: The Strategic Logic of Suicide Terrorism,' has compiled data on 315 suicide terrorism attacks from 1980-2003; he concludes that more than half of suicide attacks are unrelated to a particular religion noting that secular groups such as the LTTE in Sri Lanka and the Kurdistan Workers Party (PKK) in Turkey have conducted suicide terrorism attacks in the past. However, of the 18 groups addressed in his book on groups that are conducting suicide terrorism campaigns 16 of them are directly linked to Islam, one group (LTTE) is secular belonging to the Hindu religion and one group (Babar Khalsa International) is linked to the Sikh religion.

Since Pape's findings were published, almost all present-day suicide terrorist attacks are executed by militant Islamist groups as recorded by data produced by respectable think tanks and Government reports (this will be expanded on later in succeeding paragraphs). The number of attacks launched by militant Islamist groups surpasses suicide attacks by secular groups both in the intensity of attacks and the resultant casualties.[23] In their own words, Islamist suicide terrorists justify their acts as 'legitimate resistance' in a global holy war sanctioned by (their interpretation of) Islam against illegitimate infidel occupation of Muslim land, and anti-Muslim policies of the occupying Western powers.[24] Their ultimate goal is to restore Muslim glory and establish a universal Islamic caliphate governed by the *Sharia.*[25] Scott Atran, visiting Professor at the University of Michigan, who has written widely on suicide terrorism, claims that during 2000-2004, there were 472 suicide attacks in 22 countries killing more than 7,000 and wounding thousands. Most have been carried out by Islamist groups claiming religious motivation, also known as *jihadis.*[26]

The religious motivation of suicide terrorism cannot be ignored and must be addressed squarely in any study of suicide terrorism. Since the maximum number of present-day suicide attacks have been carried out by militant Islamist groups based on their interpretation of Islamic texts, their religious motivation must also be studied. Though Pape's research does not cover suicide terrorism after the invasion of Iraq in March 2003 (as such many of his findings now need review), he correctly predicts a further rise in suicide terrorism around the globe.[27] As suicide terrorism continues to spread to different areas and attacks become more lethal, these books will need to be updated or revised to keep up with the changes and challenges.[28]

Suicide and its Linkages with Personal Honour and Sacrifice

A brief examination of some aspects of the justification, sanction, and sometimes even the glorification of suicide *per se* in some cultures and religions of the world might help us to better understand some of the factors behind the increasing use of suicide terrorism as a form of legitimate resistance and sacrifice.[29]

Human life is considered a precious gift from God and the taking of even one's own life is forbidden by law in most countries and by all major religions. However, in some societies like those of Ancient Rome, Greece, and in Japan and Germany, suicide was an honourable and acceptable way to avoid public disgrace and humiliation while accepting full responsibility for one's failures and misdeeds. Committing suicide as the ultimate step to protect one's honour was actively encouraged under certain conditions. As explained below, some acts of suicide have even received religious sanction in ancient and medieval India.

The subject of religious motivated suicide is more complex.[30] Though the major religious traditions like Christianity, Islam, and Judaism reject suicide, martyrdom (dying or being killed for a belief or a cause that one believes is just) is actually commended as an act of selfless sacrifice. These religions distinguish between the suicide out of cowardice to escape from the pressures of living brought on by sadness, despair, an incurable illness, mental weakness or despondency, and the courageous act by another person who willingly, peacefully, and passively accepts death while defending one's religious convictions and beliefs to attain martyrdom. Christianity in particular honours passive martyrdom and many martyrs have been beatified for dying for their religion.[31] In Islam martyrdom is honoured while actively defending Islam and its beliefs. (this will be discussed later)

Ancient Rome

Centuries ago in 399 B.C., Socrates chose to commit suicide by drinking hemlock in full view of his students when he was sentenced to death on charges of atheism and corrupting the minds of the youth. Hannibal, the brilliant but unlucky Carthaginian general and statesman who defied Rome for many years during the Second and Third Punic Wars finally committed suicide in c. 183 B.C. to avoid capture by the Romans who demanded his surrender while he was in exile in Asia Minor.[32]

Both Brutus and Cassius (the assassins of Julius Caesar in 55 B.C.), killed themselves when they were defeated at the Battle of Philippi in 42 B.C. by Mark Antony and Octavian. A few years later, Mark Antony in turn fell upon his sword to avoid humiliation when he was defeated by Octavian's naval fleet at the battle of Actium in 31 B.C. Following this defeat, Mark Antony's consort, the beautiful Queen Cleopatra of Egypt also took her own life by inciting an asp (a poisonous snake) to bite her.

Roman Gladiators fought to the death all over the Roman Empire. Only the most skilled and the strongest survived in the arena. In the end only one of the fighters would be left standing. Before the signal to commence was given, gladiators would face the Emperor and proudly salute him with the words, 'We who are about to die salute you!' Though each gladiator welcomed winning in the arena and staying alive, he remained proud and fearless even in defeat and faced death with honour.

Jewish History

There are instances in Jewish history and tradition where suicide has been glorified as an honourable act. The mighty Samson committed heroic suicide to kill the Philistines who had taken him captive through deceit. After his capture, he was imprisoned, mocked and humiliated and had his eyes gouged out. He pleaded with God to assist him in his intended suicide by giving him the strength and success to pull down the pillars of the Temple of Dagon to which he was chained by the jeering Philistines. It is said that God granted Samson his suicide death wish. When Samson brought the temple crashing down upon himself, the falling debris killed him and 3,000 of the Philistine tormenters.[33]

The Old Testament also records that Saul, the first Jewish King of Israel, committed suicide by falling upon his sword to avoid capture by his enemies when he was defeated in battle against the Philistines.[34] In 73 A.D. over 900 Jewish Zealots killed themselves and their families to avoid capture and enslavement by the Roman army at the besieged fortress of Masada. Despite the strict Jewish prohibition against suicide, the collective act of self destruction at Masada has come to be regarded as a heroic sacrifice and remains a living symbol of the Israeli people's response to oppression. Modern-day Israelis vow that 'Masada shall never fall again'.

Suicide in Japan

In Japan, the *Bushido* (the way of the warriors) code of honour of the Samurai encouraged suicide by committing *hara-kiri* or *seppuku* (cutting the belly with a ceremonial sword or dagger). This method of ritual suicide was often the last honourable act of a Japanese warrior or public figure to pre-empt public humiliation and disgrace for failure or defeat in battle. For example, when the announcement of Japan's surrender to the Allies was made on August 15, 1945, over 500 Japanese committed suicide in their homes. Similar suicides took place in the military barracks, and outside the Imperial Palace to avoid the humiliation of defeat and the impending occupation. The Japanese also committed suicide in public to express their sorrow and disappointment at Japan's 'disgraceful' capitulation.[35]

Kamikaze Pilots. During the last years of the Second World War as defeat loomed close, Japan initiated very effective suicide attacks against American military targets in the Pacific. Japanese Kamikaze[36] pilots were the first to fly to certain death on 'suicide missions' and use aircraft as flying bombs when they deliberately crashed their explosive-laden bombers into American warships. As such, they were the first true suicide bombers, but they are not classified as terrorists. All their one-way volunteer missions were honourable military operations in pursuance the true *Bushido* doctrine. The planes were modified to carry additional explosives and fuel so as to cause considerable destructive damage on impact. These deliberate attempts by the Kamikaze to directly aim their bombers at US naval ships in the face of hostile anti-aircraft fire terrorised the crew onboard the American warships. There was no sure way of avoiding the oncoming explosive rigged Japanese aircraft and its pilot who was intent on certain death for the Emperor. The Kamikaze plane would explode on impact and the pilot would die in a huge fireball causing extensive damage to the warship and death or injury to its crew.[37]

The Third Reich. Field Marshal Erwin Rommel, the famous and immensely popular German commander of the *Afrika Korps* took the 'honourable' way out when he chose to commit suicide in 1944 rather than submit to an investigation by German authorities connecting him to a failed plot to assassinate Hitler. In April 1945, as the Third Reich began to collapse, Adolf Hitler committed suicide by shooting himself in his bunker, rather than be captured alive by Allied troops as the victorious Russian Army was closing in on Berlin. His mistress Eva Braun joined Hitler in his suicide pact. Joseph Goebbels, (Hitler's Minister for Propaganda), his wife, and all their children also committed suicide in the same bunker. Later, at the end of the war, Himmler and Goering also committed suicide by taking poison in 1945/ 1946.

Honourable Suicide in South Asia/India

Islamic Suicide Attacks against Colonial Powers. Religious suicide attacks have been honoured in India and South East Asia. Suicidal military attacks with no chance of success were launched as a form of offensive jihad by Muslims against colonial occupation in India, the Philippines and Indonesia. Most of these attacks were launched against a modern European power and made little military sense. Almost every attack ended in certain death and defeat for the Muslim attackers but each offensive though futile, was conducted for the sake of honour and to resist the occupation of Islamic land by non-believers.[38]

The Rajputs. Another form of collective suicide was practiced by the Hindu rulers of the princely states in Rajputana (Rajasthan) while they were at war against the Muslim armies who tried to subjugate them. The Rajputs were usually out numbered and had to endure long sieges of their desert forts until sheer force of numbers of the attackers overcame Rajput resistance. When it was thought that the defenders would surely lose, Rajput princesses and their complete entourage often committed suicide *en masse* by the act of *jauhar.* This was a form of female sacrificial suicide to preserve their honour while their men staved off the inevitable defeat by the victorious Muslim armies. As the brave but gruesome act of *jauhar* was being performed by the women, those Rajput warriors who were able, donned sacrificial saffron-coloured robes and gallantly rode out of the besieged fortress to certain death to vainly do battle with the victorious Muslim army (this act is called *saka*). In this manner, both the men and the women of the fallen garrison would ultimately die with "honour" rather than face the certain humiliation, subjugation, and dishonour of defeat.[39] These suicidal acts have been commemorated by erecting pillars and *chattris* (usually a stone or marble memorial with an umbrella–like canopy), many of which are still standing today.

The Sikhs and Martyrdom. The history of the Sikhs in India is full of instances of passive martyrdom and active resistance. The names of Guru

Arjan Singh, Guru Tegh Bahadur, and Chote Sahibzade, (Guru Gobind Singh's two sons aged 7 and 9) are the most well known and revered but several other Sikhs were tortured and killed during Mughal rule over India for refusing to give up their Sikh beliefs and convert to Islam.[40]

Sati-Female Suicide in India. At times social pressures, religious traditions and a sense of preservation of honour compelled women in India to take their own life. *Sati (*old spelling *suttee)* was a form of religious self-sacrifice usually performed under social and religious compulsion, whereby a Hindu widow committed suicide by immolating herself on her dead husband's funeral pyre. *Sati* became a somewhat accepted and expected practice in medieval India. The unfortunate woman was honoured after her death and her sins were automatically forgiven. She was sometimes even elevated to the status of a goddess. [41]

LTTE. Closer home, the LTTE go into battle or on suicide missions wearing cyanide capsules around their necks which are swallowed when capture by the enemy is imminent. Being taken alive by the enemy or the security forces is considered to be disgraceful and a security risk. Suicide is an honourable way to avoid disgrace.

The above discussion shows that the act of suicide though forbidden by law and religion, has been honoured and glorified for centuries depending on the circumstances under which it was committed. This might help us to better understand some of the motivating factors in which suicide terrorists willingly embrace death in order to kill.

Martyrdom and Struggle for Justice in Islamic History

The Holy Koran warns Muslims against committing suicide; 'Make not your own hands contribute to your destruction- life which God has made sacred.' (Koran 2:195).[42] Sunni Islam in particular views suicide as a sacrilegious act that pre-empts the will of God. The Prophet Mohammed is said to have proclaimed that a person who commits suicide will be denied Paradise and will spend his time in Hell repeating endlessly the same deed by which had ended his life on earth.

Though Islam is essentially a religion of peace, and suicide is expressly forbidden in Islam (as is the wanton killing of innocent civilians), some militant Islamists have accorded religious sanction and even glorified suicide terrorism as a self-declared *Jihad* [43] that guarantees the attacker the honoured status of martyr *(shahid)*[44] and eternal life. Further, the *shahid* is assured a place in Paradise *(jannat)*.[45] There are several verses in the Holy Koran and references in the Hadith that encourage a true Muslim to fight and die if necessary to defend the 'true religion' from attack by non-believers or apostate Muslims.[46] Islamic teachings also state that injustice and oppression must be resisted by force if necessary and that it is wrong to meekly submit to an unjust oppressor.[47] During his lifetime, the Prophet himself set a personal example in this regard. He and his followers took up the sword whenever the nascent religion of Islam was in danger of being extinguished by its enemies.[48]

To some Muslim militants, suicide operations or self-martyrdom/ sacrificial explosions are a part of *Jihad*, the holy Islamic struggle for justice. Some Islamists court death for an everlasting place in Paradise.[49] The Koran declares that those who are killed in Allah's way do not die but live forever in Paradise at Allah's side. They become *Shahid* or martyrs and the act of self sacrifice it termed *istishad*.[50] Great rewards are promised in Paradise to those who die in Allah's cause and are proclaimed martyrs.[51] It is said that a martyr's sins are forgiven and he is given the unique honour of seeing the face of Allah. *Shahids* are waited upon by 72 angels/*houris* in heaven and a martyr is able to secure a place in Paradise for 70 members of his family.[52] The first sources of the Muslim concept of martyrdom are to be found in the Koran and at the Battles of Badr and Uhud especially in the doctrine of *Jihad*.[53] The various interpretations of *Jihad* are too complex and will not be addressed here; suffice it to say that martyrdom and suicide bombings in Islam are offshoots of *Jihad* as a personal obligation of every

Muslim to battle for the downtrodden against oppression and injustice.[54]

In Islamic Shiite history, the link to sacrifice, honour and martyrdom dates back to the slaying in an unequally matched battle in 680 A.D. at Karbala (Iraq), of the Prophet's grandson Imam Hussein[55] by Yazid the new Umayyad Caliph. Hussein considered Yazid to be a Sunni usurper to the Caliphate. Though greatly outnumbered by Yazid's army, Hussein and his followers directly confronted the armies of Yazid and refused to swear allegiance to him. Hussein stood firm in his principled demand and challenged Yazid's right to the Caliphate. This demand was based on an agreement on succession made earlier between Yazid's father Muawiya of the Umayyads and Hussein's elder brother Hassan (whom Muawiya murdered). After a stand off that lasted 10 days, Hussein's small army was massacred at Karbala. Hussein's body was decapitated and desecrated but his unwavering stand and self-sacrifice against the tyrant Yazid in the face of certain death elevated Hussein to the point of veneration. He is referred to as the 'Supreme Martyr' by the Shiites worthy of future emulation. Observant Muslims both Shia and Sunni, who believe in defending the right and opposing injustice follow Hussein's example of sacrificing themselves for their cause. Their cause becomes greater than their life. Their death in a martyrdom operation is a defiant act of war and an Islamic obligation to fight injustice wherever one finds it.[56]

Militant Islamists promote an uncompromising interpretation of Islam that divides the world into Muslim and infidel. They direct the whole Muslim world to wage unremitting warfare against non-believers. The main focus of militant Islamist hatred has been against the Western world-mainly America, Israel, and its close allies including moderate Muslim countries. Muslims have traditionally viewed the West as being responsible for the historical containment, humiliation, and defeat of Islam. Islamists feel that Muslims are downtrodden because they have allowed foreign ideologies and Western influence to displace the cultural values, philosophy and the way of life that had once served as the foundation of the great Islamic civilisation.[57] For the fundamentalists, 'Islam is the only solution' to the social, economic and moral crises of the day. Resistance to the occupation of Muslim land by troops of the non-believers and their anti-Muslim policies is one of the main motivating factors for suicide terrorism.[58]

Islam has been a political religion since it was revealed, in that there is an intimate association between the religion and politics. The Koran and the life and sayings of the Prophet (the *Hadith*) is the true model for Muslims for the conduct in all matters. There were two distinct phases in the Prophet's life; one as head of the state that he had formed in Medina, and the other as a rebel against the rulers of Mecca. The Prophet of Islam founded a state and governed it. He was a statesman, general, ruler, lawmaker, judge and the Messenger of God. He imposed taxes and raised armies. He waged war and he made peace. He was ready to go to battle to set right a perceived wrong or when Islam was opposed. Therefore, politics, government, law, war and peace are all part of the Holy Law of Islam.[59] Unlike Moses the leader and saviour of the Jews and their Law Giver, and Jesus who shunned violence and taught that forgiveness, compassion, meekness were virtues to be emulated, the Prophet Muhammad taught (amongst many other lessons for peaceful co-existence and harmony), that armed resistance was a legitimate act sanctioned by religion when one was forced to fight for a just cause, overthrow an unjust ruler, or to defend Islam and Islamic lands against any form of attack.

Resurgent Islam as expressed by writers and leaders such as Khomeini, Hassan Al Banna, Qutub, Rida, Afghani, Maududi, and others expresses the desire to return to an Islamic society governed by Islamic law and ruled by an Islamic state.[60] The radical or fundamentalist Islamic group that uses terrorist acts to achieve its ultimate goals is a relatively new phenomenon with very deep roots.[61] It is somewhat different from other forms of terrorism in that it rejects all the contemporary ideologies in their various forms. It sees itself with no other option but to take control in the name of Islam, or die in the attempt.[62] Considering itself as an expression of Islamic revival that must lead to the conquest of the entire globe by the 'true faith' - it believes in the dictum that 'the end justifies the means' (including acts of suicide terrorism).

End Notes To Chapter 1

1. Suicide Terrorism has killed hundreds of soldiers and civilians in places as far apart as India, Sri Lanka, Israel, Afghanistan, Saudi Arabia, Kenya, Morocco, Algeria, Tunisia, Yemen, Pakistan, Philippines, Turkey, Indonesia, Iraq, United Kingdom, United States, and Russia (including Chechnya). The term 'suicide terrorism' has been accepted for usage in Terrorism Studies and research.

2. International pressure and Pakistani promises based on General Musharraf's January 12, and May 27, 2002 speeches to act against terrorists on its soil defused the tense situation. India pulled back its troops in October 2002 without going to war.

3. See Text of the Proclamation of Emergency declared by General Pervez Musharraf on November 3, 2007 reproduced in *The Asian Age,* (Mumbai), 4 November 2007, p.3., and 'Emergency Order Blames Militancy, Judiciary,' *ibid.*

4. For a comprehensive background see David C. Rapport, 'Fear and Trembling: Terrorism in Three Religious Traditions', *American Political Science Review*, Vol. 78, September, 1984 pp 658-677. For the subsequent upsurge in religion-backed terrorism see Bruce Hoffman, 'Holy Terror: The Implications of Terrorism Motivated by a Religious Imperative,' (RAND Paper P-7834, 1993); and Mark Juergensmeyer, 'Terror in the Mind of God: The Global Rise of Religious Violence,' (University of California Press, 2000).

5. Scott Atran, 'Trends in Suicide Terrorism: Sense and Nonsense', Paper presented in Sicily in August 2004 at World Federation of Scientists Permanent Monitoring Panel on Terrorism.

6. Considered to be mainly a Shiite phenomenon based on the martyrdom of Imam Hussein at Karbala (Iraq) in the 7th Century, the ideology and practice of Suicide Terrorism has also been effectively adopted by Sunni Muslims, and other secular and Islamist groups. It

poses a global threat against which no country has yet devised foolproof countermeasures.

7. This aspect is well covered in Mohammed Hafez, 'Suicide Bombers in Iraq: The Strategy and Ideology of Martyrdom,' (United States Institute of Peace Press, Washington DC, 2007), and Robert J. Bunker and John P. Sullivan, 'Suicide Bombings in Operation Iraqi Freedom,' *Military Review*, January-February, 2005 pp 69-79, reprint (originally published in September 2004 as paper No. 46 W by the Institute of Land Warfare).

8. See Robert Fisk, 'Five Years of Suicide Bombings in Iraq', *The Independent*, March 20, 2008 at <http://www.alternet.org/story/79779/>.

9. Jason Straziuso, *Associated Pres* in, 'Afghanistan's Deadly War', The *Oregonian*, (Portland, OR), July 01, 2008 p. A5.

10. Some examples are such as the Liberation Tigers of Tamil Eelam (LTTE) in Sri Lanka, the Kurdish Workers Party (PKK) in Turkey, Islamic Resistance Movement (HAMAS) in Israel, Hezbollah in Lebanon, Sunni and Shiite groups in Iraq and in Pakistan, Al Qaeda–linked Islamists in Afghanistan, Saudi Arabia, and South East Asia, Jamaah Islamiyah in Indonesia, Chechen groups in Russia and Pakistani terrorists operating in the Indian state of Jammu and Kashmir (henceforth shortened to Kashmir) from the Lashkar e Toiba and Jaish e Muhammad. Some of these groups will be discussed in greater detail in subsequently.

11. RAND-MIPT at <www.rand.org/ise/projects/terrorismdatabase>, US State Department National Counter Terrorism Center (NCTC) dated 13 April 2007 and 28 April 2008 at <www.state.gov/s/ct/rls/crt/2006/82739.htm>, South Asia Terrorism Portal at <www.satp.org>.

12. The suicide car bombing killed 41 (including 4 Indians), and injured at least 141 (all of them Afghan nationals). It was the deadliest attack in Kabul since Op Enduring Freedom was launched in October 2001.

13. The word 'martyr' comes from the Greek '*martus*' - a true witness (of Christ or the religion). The word 'sacrifice' comes from the Latin '*sacer*' (sacred or holy) + '*facere*' (to make) which means 'to make holy or sacred'.

14. Boaz Ganor (Ed), 'Countering Suicide Terrorism' (Institute of Counter Terrorism, Herzliya, 2000)

15. This is very different from high risk (suicidal) commando missions undertaken as part of a military objective, whereby the chances of returning alive are very slim. In all such

special military missions every effort is made by commanders to plan for the safe return/ extraction of its operatives even under enemy fire.

16. This view is also taken by noted suicide bomber psychologist Anne Speckhard. See her definition of Chechen suicide terrorists in Anne Speckhard and Khapta Ahkmedova, 'The Making of a Martyr: Chechen Suicide Terrorism,' *Studies in Conflict and Terrorism*, No. 29, 2006,pp. 429-492.

17 . Quoted by Ami Pedahzur and Arie Perliger during their research at National Security Studies Center data base at University of Haifa and includes those killed and injured. Also see Ami Pedahzur, 'Suicide Terrorism', (Polity Press, 2004). I am thankful to Prof Pedahzur for sharing the manuscript of his book with me.

18. Boaz Ganor, 'The Rationality of the Islamic Radical Suicide Attack Phenomenon', Institute of Counter Terrorism, Herzliya website at <http://ict.org.il/apage/printv/ 11290.php>.

19. There are many other advantages of suicide terrorism over 'normal' terrorism. See Boaz Ganor, *Suicide Attacks in Israel*, in 'Countering Suicide Terrorism', International Policy Institute for Counter Terrorism, (ICT Herzliya 2001)pp.134-145, and Robert Pape, 'Dying to Win: The Strategic Logic of Suicide Terrorism', (Random, USA, 2005).

20. 'Suicide Terrorism on the Rise Worldwide, Experts Say', US Department of State, October 19, 2007 at <http;//usinfo.state.gov/utils>.

21. Suicide bombings took place in Amman, Riyadh, Istanbul, Casablanca, Sana'a, Algiers, Islamabad, Manila, Karachi, Pakistan's North West Frontier Province, Tunis, Jakarta and Bali.

22. Some of these are, Robert Pape, 'Dying to Win: the Strategic Logic of Suicide Terrorism,' (Random House, New York, 2005); Anne Marie Oliver and Paul F. Steinberg, 'The Road to Martyrs' Square: A Journey into the World of the Suicide Bomber,' (Oxford University Press, New York, 2005); Mia Bloom, 'Dying to Kill: The Allure of Suicide Terror,' (Columbia University Press, 2005); Barbara Victor, 'An Army of Roses: Inside the World of Palestinian Women Suicide Bombers,' (Rodale Books, 2003); Christoph Reuter, 'My Life is a Weapon: A History of Modern Suicide Bombing,' (Manas/Princeton University Press, Delhi ,2004); and Farhad Khosrokhavar, 'Suicide Bombers: Allah's New Martyrs,' (Pluto Press, London, 2005).

23. Figures given out annually by research establishments like RAND, Country Reports

and the National Counter Terrorism Center, State Department USA, Patterns of Global Terrorism reports by the US, IISS Reports London, Brookings Institution Reports and analyses.

24. For example see Shaul Shay, 'The Endless Jihad', (The International Counter Terrorism Policy Institute, Herzliya, 2002), John Esposito, The Islamic Threat, Myth or Reality, (Oxford Press, New York, 1999), Amir Mir, 'The True Face of Jehadis: Inside Pakistan's Network of Terror, (Roli Books, New Delhi, 2006)

25. See 'Current Trends in Islamist Ideology', Volumes1-4 (Hudson Institute, Washington DC, 2005) where quotes from Islamist ideologues are recorded. Another example is the formation of the *World Islamic Front against Jews and Crusaders* and Osama bin Laden's 1988 declaration of a Global Jihad against Jews and Crusaders.

26. Quoted from Scott Atran, 'Moral Logic and Growth of Suicide Terrorism', *Washington Quarterly* 29:2 2006, pp. 127-147.

27. Robert Pape, "Dying to Win: The Strategic Logic of Suicide Terrorism", (Random House, New York, 2005)

28. This aspect has been very well discussed especially with reference to Robert Pape's book 'Dying to Win: The Strategic Logic of Suicide Terrorism' op cit, Scott Atran, 'The Moral Logic and Growth of Suicide Terrorism', *Washington Quarterly,* 29:2, 2006, pp. 127-147. Also see Assaf Moghadam, 'Suicide Terrorism, Occupation, and the Globalization of Martyrdom: A Critique of Dying to Win', *Studies in Conflict and Terrorism* 29; pp. 707-729, 2006 wherein some of Pape's finding are challenged by the author.

29. For a comprehensive argument on 'Suicide' see 'The Encyclopaedia of Religion', M. Eliade, Ed in Chief, Macmillan, 1987, Vol. 14, pp125-130, and 'The Encyclopaedia of Philosophy', Paul Edwards, Ed in chief, Macmillan, 1967, Vol. 17, pp 43-45. Also see Emile Durkheim, 'Suicide: A Study in Sociology,' (New York, Free Press, 1957) where Durkheim has classified different types of suicide in his ground breaking research on the subject.

30. There is an abundance of literature on the subject. For some references see, David C. Rapoport, 'Fear and Trembling in Three Religious Traditions,' *American Political Science Review*, Vol. 78, No. 3, September 1984, pp. 668-672, Bruce Hoffman, 'Holy Terror: The Implications of Terrorism Motivated by a Religious Motive,' RAND, Santa Monica, Paper P 7834, 1993, Mark Juergenmeyer, 'Terror in the Mind of God: The Global Rise of

Religious Violence,' (University of California Press, 2000), and Amir Taheri, 'Holy Terror: The Inside Story of Islamic Terrorism,' (Hutchinson, London, 1987).

31. For example: Joan of Arc, St. Stephen, St. Peter, St Paul to name a few.

32. Hannibal (247-183B.C.) was a sworn enemy of Rome. He executed brilliant military victories against the Romans by first crossing the Pyrenees and then the Alps into Italy, and routing the Roman Army at Lake Trasimene and Cannae. He also threatened the city of Rome itself. Lack of resources and Roman resilience forced him to withdraw to Carthage where he was defeated at Zama in 202 B.C. He went into voluntary exile, but continued to defy Roman power until he committed suicide by taking poison to avoid capture by the Romans in northern Turkey c. 183 B.C. He was aged 64.

33. The Bible (Old Testament), Judges 16 and 17. Samson's strength lay in his hair. He was captured by the Philistines through Delilah who had lured him and drugged him to sleep. The Philistines imprisoned him, gouged out his eyes, and shaved off his hair to deprive him of his gigantic power. As his hair grew, his strength returned. Samson called out to God and asked that he be allowed to die with the Philistines during his self-orchestrated suicide.

34. The Bible (Old Testament), Book of Samuel 1:17.

35. Mass collective suicide has also committed by cults such as Heaven's Gate followers in USA (39 killed themselves in 1997), and the Jim Jones followers in Jonestown, French Guyana where over 914 people including 214 children killed themselves in 1978, but do not form part of this study.

36. The word means 'divine wind'. In 1281, a fortuitous typhoon dispersed and damaged a Mongol invasion fleet threatening Japan from the West.

37. See Raymond Lamont-Brown, 'Kamikaze: Japan's Suicide Samurai', (Cassell, London, 1997 reprint 2000). Kamikaze pilots were all volunteers and went through a religious purification ritual in addition to military training. The attacks first started in October 1944 at the Battle of Leyte Gulf and continued till the end of the War in August 1945. Over 2940 missions were launched. Kamikaze attacks sank 34 US naval ships and damaged hundreds others. At Okinawa, kamikaze attacks inflicted the greatest losses ever suffered by the US Navy in a single battle by killing almost 5000 men. Admiral Takijiro Onishi, the 'father of the Kamikaze' committed *seppuku* on 15 August 1945, the day when Japan announced its surrender. Admiral Ugaki, led the last remaining 11 dive bombers of the 701 Air Group from Kyushu to a futile kamikaze attack against Okinawa. Both commanders

apologised to the memories of the brave pilots before them who had fallen like 'cherry blossoms' for the glory and honour of Japan. The controversial Yakusuni shrine in Tokyo still preserves the relics of the Kamikaze and honours Japan's war dead.

38. This aspect has been very well covered by Stephen F. Dale, 'Religious Suicide in Islamic Asia: Anti Colonial Terrorism in India, Indonesia and the Philippines,' *Journal of Conflict Resolution*, Vol. 32 No.1. March 1988, pp 37-59 and Iqtidar Alam Khan, 'Anti-Colonial Resistance and the Jihad Movement of Nineteenth Century India', in 'War and Peace in Islam', (Harman Publications/Delhi Policy Group Seminar New Delhi, 2002).

39. In 1303, Rani Padmini is said to have led over 30,000 women to commit suicide (*jauhar*) at Chitor when Alahuddin Khilji stormed the fort. In 1535 when Chitor was about to fall to Bahadur Shah's Muslim army from Gujarat, over 32,000 women committed *jauhar* and 13,000 Rajput defenders rode out to certain death wearing saffron robes as a mark of sacrifice. Chitor was once again sacked in 1568, this time by the Mughal Emperor Akbar, when it is said that over 8,000 men committed *saka,* 30,000 were killed, and thousands of women committed *jauhar* to avoid dishonour.

40. Sikh martyrs are revered even today and sometimes referred to as 'shahids'. For a good account of this subject see Louis E Fenech 'Martyrdom in the Sikh Tradition: Playing the Game of Love,' (Oxford University Press, New Delhi, 2000). For the history and brief biographies of Sikh martyrs see 'Great Sikh Martyrs' at <www.sikh-history.com/sikhhist/martyrs/nojava.html>. Recently, even Sant Bhinderwale the Sikh militant who fortified the Golden Temple and was killed in 1984 with his followers during the Indian Army attack on the Golden temple in Amritsar was declared a martyr by a section of the Sikhs in Punjab.

41. *Sati* (meaning 'chaste' or 'virtuous woman' in Sanskrit) has first been mentioned as a Hindu custom in the ancient Indian text of the epic Mahabharata. It was practiced in almost the whole of India at various times; see *The Hindus: Encyclopaedia of Hinduism*, Subodh Kapoor, Ed., Vol. 4., (New Delhi, Cosmos Publications 2000), pp. 1625-26. For a discussion of *sati* as a form of suicide and its prevalence in India, see the *Encyclopaedia of Religion* note 13 above and *The New Encyclopaedia Britannica, Micropaedia*, 15th Edition, Vol. 11(1985) pp.359 and 420. For a well-researched article on *sati* and on *jauhar,* see Julia Leslie, "Suttee or Sati: Victim or Victor?" in David Arnold and Peter Robb (Eds), *Institutions and Ideologies: A SOAS Reader*, (UK: Curzon Press, 1993), pp. 45-63. The British (Lord William Bentinck) outlawed the *sati* in 1829 as it was considered an act of suicide. The early Mughal emperors Humayun and Akbar too tried to prohibit the practice of *sati* as Islam expressly forbids suicide. Though illegal in India, incidents of *sati* are

reported from time to time. The last recorded act of *sati* that received a lot of media attention was that of an 18 year old Rajput woman, Roop Kanwar on 04 September 1987. As per *Time* magazine of September 28, 1987, Roop Kanwar was considered a goddess by her village and almost $160,000 had been collected in voluntary donations to build a shrine in her honour as a deity. In August 2002, a 65-year woman committed suttee in the state of Madhya Pradesh. As per some media reports the act was premeditated, voluntary, and in full public view.

42. Suicide is prohibited in the Koran which states, 'Make not your own hands contribute to your destruction; Life which God has made sacred.' (Surah 2:195). Sunni Islam views any form of suicide as a sacrilegious act that defies and pre-empts the will of God. Islamists point out that normal suicide is the last voluntary act of a weak and despondent person who is either unable or unwilling to face the challenges and pressures of day to day living. In contrast, they emphasise, that '*self-martyrdom*' is the deliberate offensive act of a *holy warrior* engaged in a *Jihad*. Despite these divergent views, suicide attacks encouraged by radical Islamic extremists continue unabated with renewed vigour, drawing more and more volunteers from all over the Islamic world.

43. There is a large volume of written work on the meaning and interpretation of the word '*jihad*' by various authors. In this paper, the interpretation by most militant Islamists that *Jihad* is an obligatory offensive holy Muslim war to defend and preserve the true Islam against all enemies of the 'straight path of Islam' will be adhered to. Also see Michael A Knapp, 'The Concept and Practice of Jihad in Islam', *Parameters*, Spring 2003 pp. 82-94, and Jonah Winters, 'Martyrdom in Jihad', at website <www.Jihadfn.htm>.

44. For a detailed argument on 'Martyrdom' see *The Encyclopaedia of Religion*, M. Eliade, Ed-in-Chief, (Macmillan, 1987), Vol. 9, pp 230-237 and *The Encyclopaedia of Islam* New Edition, *Shahid* pp.203-206. Also see A. Ezzati, "The Concept of Martyrdom in Islam," Teheran University, *Al Serat*, Vol 12, 1986 and Aluma Solnick, "The Shuhada Cult of Martyrdom in *'Islamic Jihad* ", at website < www.memri.com >. The term is now loosely used to honour anyone killed on the battlefield or during a national struggle; *i.e.* Indian soldiers killed in the May-July 1999 conflict against Pakistani aggressors in Kargil are referred to as 'Kargil Martyrs'. Freedom fighters killed in India's freedom struggle like Bhagat Singh are also referred to as *shahid*. Indira Gandhi who was assassinated in 1984 while in office is also called a 'martyr'.

45. The Koran declares that 'those who are killed in Allah's way do not die but live forever in paradise at Allah's side' (Koran 3:169). They become *shahid* or martyrs. Islam

valorizes and glorifies the death of a martyr as a witness to the 'straight path' of Islam. The Koran says, "Wars come to provide martyrs and that God may prove those who believe. Paradise is only to be attained when God knows who will really strive and endure." It is believed that this concept of 'battlefield martyrs' was first stated by the Prophet Muhammad at the battle of Uhud (in 625 AD) when his uncle Hamza was killed in battle and was declared a martyr. The 70 Muslims who were killed that day were also given the status of martyrs and entered Paradise.

46.   For example, Koran 3:169 translates as: "You must not think that those who were slain in the cause of Allah are dead. They are alive, and well provided for by their Lord."

47.   Koran 2:216- 'Fighting is ordered for you even though you dislike it and it may be that you dislike a thing that is good for you and like a thing that is bad for you. Allah knows but you do not know.' Also Koran 4:75 ' And why should you not fight in the cause of God and (for) all those who being weak are ill-treated and oppressed... whose rulers are oppressors....'

48.   For one account of the Prophet's life see, Martin Lings, 'Muhammad: His Life Based on the Earliest Sources', (Inner Traditions, Rochester, 1983). For an account of his battles and references to the Koranic verses for battle see Brigadier S.K. Malik, 'The Quranic Concept of War,' (Himalayan Books, New Delhi, 1986).

49.   For one treatment of Jihad see Richard Bonney, 'Jihad from Quran to bin Laden' (Palgrave Macmillan, New York, 2004). Also see Reuven Firestone, 'Jihad: The Origin of Holy War in Islam,' (Oxford University Press, New York, 1999).

50.   For a study of martyrdom and suicide terrorism see Hugh Barlow, 'Dead for Good: Martyrdom and the Rise of the Suicide Bomber', Paradigm Publishers, London, 2007). The book covers different aspects of martyrdom in Christianity, Islam, Judaism, Sikhism, and the Japanese Kamikaze.

51.   For the privileges of those who fall in battle and are declared martyrs as recorded in the Koran and Islamic texts, see Eitan Kohlberg, *The Encyclopaedia of Islam*, vol. 9 (Leiden: E.J. Brill, 1960), s.v. "shahid."

52.   See David Bukay, 'The Religious Foundations of Suicide Bombings; Islamist Ideology', *Middle East Quarterly* Fall 2006 at <www.meforum.org/article/1003> for quotations from the Koran and the Hadith on the subject.

53.   See A.G. Noorani, 'Islam and Jihad,' (Left Word Books, New Delhi, 2002), and Richard

Bonney, 'Jihad; From Quran to bin Laden,' (Palgrave Macmillan, New York, 2004).

54. To understand the concept of suicide terrorism and Islam see, Shaul Shay, 'The Shahids: Islam and Suicide Attacks,' (Transaction Publishers, London, 2004); and Raphael Israeli, 'Islamikaze: Manifestations of Islamic Martyrology,' (Frank Cass, London, 2003). However, both authors have focused mainly on suicide attacks in Israel.

55. Shiite Muslims take their name from Hussein's father, The Iman Ali, who was cousin and son-in-law of the Prophet. Ali was assassinated in Najaf, Iraq in 661 AD.

56. Also see Christoph Reuter, 'My Life is a Weapon', (Manas Publications, New Delhi, 2005)

57. See Fareed Zakaria, 'Islam and the West: The Roots of Rage', *Newsweek,* Oct 15, 2001 pp10-27, and 'Why Do They Hate America?' *The Sunday Times* (London), 23 Sep 2001. For the privileges of martyrs who fall in battle, see Eitan Kohlberg, *The Encyclopedia of Islam*, vol. 9 (Leiden: E.J. Brill, 1960), s.v. "shahid."

58. This argument is expanded in Robert Pape, 'Dying to Win: The Strategic Logic of Suicide Terrorism', (Random House, USA, 2005).

59. Bernard Lewis, 'The Return to Islam', *Middle Eastern Review*, Vol. XII No. 1, Fall 1979, pp. 23-31.

60. For details of the concept and historical background see Asghar Ali Engineer, 'The Islamic State', (Vikas Publishing House, New Delhi, 1994).

61. See Shumel Bar, 'The Religious Sources of Islamic Terrorism', *Policy Review*, No. 125, June/July 2004.

62. Ajai Sahni, 'Extremist Islamist Terror and Subversion in South Asia', Paper presented at International Seminar organised by The Institute for Conflict Management, New Delhi in October 2001, titled 'The Global Threat of Terror: Ideological, Material and Political Linkages'

CHAPTER 2

GROUPS ASSOCIATED WITH SUICIDE TERRORISM AND DISTURBING TRENDS

To understand Suicide terrorism it would be helpful to know a little bit about groups that have refined this deadly method of terrorism, and what motivates them. The majority of the groups have their roots in West Asia (Middle East) though suicide terrorism is not exclusively a Middle Eastern or Islamic phenomenon. Currently most suicide terrorism attacks are being launched in the Middle East and South/South West Asia. A brief overview of some groups associated with suicide terrorism/Martyrdom operations as part of their strategy is given below.

Brief Overview of Some Suicide Terrorist Groups

The Assassins (Fidayeen)

♦ This Shiite group was formed in the 11 century A.D. by Hassan Sabbah in Iran. His aim was to kill unjust rulers of the Seljuk Turks who were in power at the time by using dedicated killers at close range who would kill in public view to spread terror and fear.[1] They called themselves *fidayeen* and were willing to sacrifice their life for Islam. Later, they also attacked Crusaders and other unjust Muslim rulers. They always used a dagger as the weapon of execution and killed at close quarters. After the attack, they expected to be killed by the guards in return and did not attempt to run away. To be captured alive was considered a disgrace. The influence of the *fidayeen* was felt in Syria and throughout the Islamic world for two centuries. In the 13th century their power extended as far as Karakorum, the capital of the Mongol empire. The Mongols targeted them for destruction in 1256 and within a year they were eradicated. The *fidayeen* were also called *hashshashin* as it was thought that the 'holy killers' were under the influence of opiates or hashish to willingly undertake such suicidal missions.[2]

♦ This group has inspired the ideology of martyrdom and self-sacrifice of the *fidai*- a person willing to sacrifice one's life while committing a righteous act against an oppressor.

The Iranian Revolution and the *Bassiji*

♦ During the Iran-Iraq War in the 1980s, Ayatollah Khomeini gave religious sanction and encouragement to thousands of unarmed boys and men to charge Iraqi gun positions by walking unarmed through deep mine fields in human waves wearing the keys of Paradise round their necks. They were told that they were fighting a jihad against Iraq to regain the holy Shiite city of Karbala (the site of Imam Hussein martyrdom) in Iraq from Saddam Hussein. When they were killed by gunfire or blown up on Iraqi mines, martyrdom and place in Paradise were assured. Their war cry was "Ya Karbala! Ya Hussein, Ya Khomeini!" The Iranian counter offensives were also named after Karbala (for example Karbala V or VI) and they were convinced that their death would result in martyrdom.[3] Following the Iranian revolution and during the Iran-Iraq war, Ayatollah Khomeini was the first Muslim leader in modern times to encourage suicide/sacrificial explosions in a holy Islamic war to attain martyrdom and assure the dead a place in Paradise. Khomeini reiterated that "The Tree of Islam can only grow if it is constantly fed with the blood of martyrs".[4]

♦ In the current standoff between Iran and the U.S., regarding Iran's nuclear programme, this concept of human wave suicide attacks and martyrdom has been revived by the current Iranian regime. Iran claims that over 40,000 suicide bombers are ready to sacrifice themselves against American and British targets if the United States dared to attack Iran.[5]

Hezbollah (Party of God)

♦ A powerful Shiite military and political group that was formed to resist the Israeli invasion of Lebanon in 1982. It adopted the Iranian ideology of sacrificing one's life for the cause. It was the first to use suicide terrorism as a strategic weapon against US, Israeli, and French troops deployed in Lebanon in 1983 and develop it as a weapon of legitimate resistance against Israeli occupation of Lebanon and Jerusalem.[6]

♦ Hezbollah changed tactics to guerrilla warfare from 1986 when Israel withdrew from most parts of Lebanon in 1985. It is worth noting that during the July 2006 war with Israel, the Hezbollah did not resort to suicide terrorism but fought a successful asymmetrical war with Israel which included firing long and short range rockets on Israeli cities and causing attrition on Israel's ground offensive.

♦ The last suicide attack against Israel took place in 1999 and Hezbollah took credit for the final withdrawal of Israeli troops in May 2000.[7] Hezbollah's successful suicide terrorism campaign was adopted by many other groups such as HAMAS, LTTE, PKK, and Al Qaeda.

Kurdistan Workers Party (PKK) in Turkey

♦ The party was formed in 1978 in Turkey, but resorted to terrorism in 1984. It followed a Marxist-Leninist ideology based on Kurdish ethno-nationalism. It owed allegiance to just one leader Abdullah Ocalan. Though a secular organisation, it used Islam as a rallying point from time to time. Most Kurds are Muslims. The PKK's political aim is a separate state for Kurds in South Eastern Turkey.

- PKK stopped using suicide terrorism in July 1999 after the capture of Ocalan. During the period 1984-1999, the PKK carried out 15 suicide attacks against varied targets such as the police, political figures and soft targets in Turkey. It was one of the first groups to use women. Out of 15 suicide attackers, 11 were young women aged 17-27 yrs. PKK called themselves *fidayeen* and considered that any form of violence is legitimate to gain an independent state.

- Their operations were a combination of guerrilla warfare and suicide terrorism. They have safe havens in Northern Iraq and are also organised in parts of Iran. They also used to have bases in Syria. The tempo of suicide terrorism was related to Abdullah Ocalan's capture and his trial.[8] The PKK has now resorted to guerrilla warfare from bases in Northern Iraq and is the target of frequent air strikes and ground offensives from Turkey's military. Over 12,000 civilians and soldiers have been killed and over 32,000 PKK militants have lost their lives to date.[9]

LTTE in Sri Lanka

- Aim of the LTTE is to establish Tamil Eelam (a homeland) in North East Sri Lanka. The suicide cadre are called Black Tigers.

- This group carried out its first suicide attack in 1987. It introduced suicide terrorism after watching the success of Hezbollah in Lebanon, and refined it to suit its own purpose and cause; a Tamil homeland in North and Eastern Sri Lanka. The group has carried out over 240 suicide attacks since 1987 killing over 60,000 persons. It was one of the leading organisations in suicide terrorism until overtaken by Al Qaeda and other militant Islamist groups in Iraq. The suicide vest and explosive belt so commonly used by Palestinian groups and suicide bombers today is thought to have been designed by the LTTE (to fit its female cadres). Suicide terrorism operations are conducted by the LTTE only in Sri Lanka. It has financial support of the Sri Lankan Diaspora abroad and from illegal trade and smuggling.[10]

♦ The LTTE has conducted just one suicide terrorism operation in India-the Rajiv Gandhi assassination in South India in 1991. However, while the Indian Peace Keeping Force (IPKF) was deployed in Sri Lanka from 1987-1990, no suicide attacks were executed against the Indian Army.

♦ A cease fire with the Sri Lankan government since Sep 2002 (during which no suicide attacks were launched) finally broke down in January 2008, and the LTTE commenced suicide attacks again. Its operatives carry cyanide capsules to commit suicide in case of imminent capture or failure of an explosive device. This reflects the spirit of sacrifice and martyrdom inculcated during indoctrination of the LTTE. Though a Hindu group, it does not use Hinduism as a motivating factor. It is based on ethno-nationalism and past glory of the Chola Empire. Its symbols are taken from Hindu/Tamil mythology and history of the Chola Empire.

♦ LTTE was devoted to its leader Vellupillai Prabhakaran, and as such is a leader-centric organisation.[11] The LTTE has elevated Martyrdom to an act of heroism and valour. It has a large female cadre which also carry out suicide attacks in a big way.[12] The LTTE has a small air wing and a maritime wing. Suicide cadres have attacked Sri Lankan Naval ships and civilian vessels with explosive laden boats.

♦ The October 2000 attack on the USS Cole killing 17 US Navy personnel off the coast of Yemen is thought to have been executed after Al Qaeda viewed LTTE videos of its successful maritime suicide attacks against the Sri Lankan Navy.

Al Qaeda

- This group is by far the most innovative and successful Islamist suicide terrorist organisation. It was founded in 1988/89 in Afghanistan. It gained momentum after the American invasion of Iraq in 1991 and the basing of US troops in Saudi Arabia.[13]

- Its main plank is the International Islamic Front for Jihad against Jews and Crusaders launched in 1998 by Osama bin Laden. Suicide attacks resulting in mass casualties is its hallmark and includes simultaneous attacks and multiple bombings on far flung targets. It is virulently against the US and Israel and also against moderate Muslim countries that support the US such as Saudi Arabia, Iraq, Jordan, Afghanistan, Turkey, Morocco, Egypt, Pakistan, Algeria, Tunisia, and Yemen.[14]

- Some of the Pakistani suicide terrorist groups like the *Lashkar e Taiba* have signed on as part of Al Qaeda's world wide jihad. Al Qaeda has been involved either directly or indirectly in every major suicide bombing all over the world. Splinter groups of Al Qaeda have come up with names such as Al Qaeda in Iraq, Al Qaeda in Europe, Al Qaeda in the Islamic Maghreb, Al Qaeda in Pakistan, and Al Qaeda in Saudi Arabia.[15] Al Qaeda has inspired several terrorist groups around the worlds like the Afghan and Pakistan Taliban, *Lashkar e Toiba and Jaish e Muhammad* which also execute lethal suicide terrorism attacks.

- Though some of its leaders have been killed or captured, the organisation has shown resilience to survive and carry out a 'leaderless jihad'. Osama bin Laden has been on the run since October 2001, and is believed to be hiding in the lawless tribal areas along the Pakistan-Afghanistan border.

- First major suicide attack was the twin bombing of the US Embassies in Kenya and Tanzania in 1998. It carried out the catastrophic 9/11 suicide attacks against the US, and a series of lethal bombings around the world.[16] Al Qaeda's ideology of a Global jihad has made suicide terrorism attacks a global phenomenon.[17]

Chechen Terrorist Groups

- These groups are based on Islamic and nationalist ideology demanding independence from Russia to establish an Islamic Chechnya. Chechen Islamists have resorted to suicide terrorism to resist alleged atrocities from Russian Army during its counter terrorism operations and press their demand for independence. Black Widows suicide cadre of females were formed to take revenge for the Chechen men killed by the Russian Army.

- Over 112 suicide bombers have taken part in about 28 suicide terror operations since June 2000.[18]

- Their operations are not limited to Chechnya but have included suicide terrorism attacks in the heart of Moscow. In October 2002, 40 suicide terrorists (including 19 women) took over 800 people hostage at a theatre in Moscow threatening to blow up the theatre. The Russian government refused to negotiate and launched a hostage rescue operation (using gas) killing all the terrorists before they could blow themselves up. 129 hostages also died in the rescue.

- In September 2004, over 1120 school children and adults were taken hostage by 32 suicide terrorists in Beslan (North Ossetia). In the rescue operation over 330 hostages were killed including 30 terrorists. Chechen Islamists have also carried out several truck suicide bombings, political assassinations and also blown up a Russian aircraft in midair using women suicide bombers. In

December 2002, 57 were killed in Grozny, in May 2003, 59 were killed in truck suicide bomb in Moscow, in May 2003, 14 were killed in Grozny by female bombers, in June 2003, 18 soldiers were killed by a female suicide bomber dressed as an Army Nurse on a military bus.

♦   Russia's firm resolve in not giving in to Chechen suicide terrorism despite heavy civilian casualties during rescue operations, has forced the Chechens to look for a political solution. The number of suicide terrorism attacks has dropped dramatically since the Beslan attack. Russian Special Forces have also been very successful in eliminating the senior leadership of the Chechen terrorist groups. [19]

HAMAS (Islamic Resistance Movement) and other Palestinian Groups

♦   HAMAS is a Sunni Islamist group formed in 1988 as an offshoot of Muslim Brotherhood. HAMAS (which means 'zeal' in Arabic) is an acronym for *Harkat al Maqawama al Islamiya*. It has a militant Islamist agenda to free Palestine from Israeli occupation. Its hallmark is suicide terrorist attacks inside Israel using human bombs strapped with explosives. It gained its expertise from Hezbollah operations in Lebanon after Israel had expelled HAMAS operatives to Lebanon in December 1992. [20] HAMAS was elected to government in the Palestinian territories in January 2006. However, it has not been recognised by major world powers because of its militant Islamist agenda and resistance against Israel.

♦   Its Charter states the "the Prophet is the model, the Koran its constitution, and Jihad in the name of Allah as a way of   life." It has a political and military wing and also carries out laudable social assistance programmes mainly in the Gaza Strip.

◆ The *Izz al Din (Izzedine) al Kassam* brigades conduct suicide attacks. In addition to HAMAS, Palestinian Islamic Jihad, and Al Aqsa Martyrs Brigade (an off shoot of the secular Fatah) have been carrying out suicide terrorism attacks against Israel. Israeli retaliations using disproportionate force which result in avoidable civilian causalities have fuelled more suicide attacks by HAMAS. HAMAS claims that it has the legitimate right to resist Israeli occupation of Palestine and fight against Israel's humiliating policies against Palestinians by all means possible including martyrdom operations.

◆ Though suicide terrorism consisted of only 1 percent of all Palestinian attacks from September 2000-August 2002 they caused 44 percent of all Israeli casualties.

◆ Since 2003 suicide attacks have steadily reduced as Israeli counter terrorism actions took effect. Targeted killings, house demolitions/ deportations, construction of the separation barrier and effective penetration of the organization have decimated Palestinian groups. Israeli counter measures have severely reduced their effectiveness to launch any suicide attacks inside Israel.

Suicide Terrorism in the Iraq War

◆ At the beginning of the war, 4000 suicide terrorists claimed to be ready to attack the invading US forces in March 2003. The *Saddam e Fedayeen* were though to be a potent suicide terrorist group. When the invasion began, the expected suicide attacks did not materialise and Baghdad fell sooner than expected. Suicide bombings were unheard of before the March 2003 invasion of Iraq.

◆ However, as the war dragged on, suicide bombers of Sunni groups backed by Al Qaeda attacked the United Nations offices, Red Cross workers, several soft targets including embassies and the coalition forces inside Iraq. Suicide bombers also attacked targets in countries that supported (or did not oppose) the invasion such as Turkey, Morocco, Tunisia and Saudi Arabia or had troops in Iraq such as UK and Spain.[21] Iraq leads the world as the county with the most suicide attacks to date (though insurgent attacks have dropped in number since the 2007 US troop 'surge').

♦ Suicide bombers usually use explosive laden cars or trucks for maximum effect. In one case a suicide bomber detonated himself under a chlorine-filled truck which turned into a devastating chemical bomb.[22]

♦ Iraqi political leaders and Iraqi security forces are also being targeted. Shia mosques, Shia pilgrims, public places like markets, recruiting centres, schools, hospitals, and festive gatherings were also attacked resulting in heavy loss of innocent lives. These attacks increased after the elections gave the Shiites a majority vote. These suicide attacks aim to force US and foreign troops to withdraw from Iraq and re-establish Sunni rule over Iraq.[23]

♦ Iraq has now been consumed by sectarian violence mainly between the Sunni and Shiite factions. Groups such as Al Qaeda in Iraq, Ansar al Islam, Ansar al Sunna, Tawhid wal Jihad, Al Quds Brigade, elements of the Mahdi Army and foreign fighters inducted by Iran, Syria and Saudi Arabia are creating havoc in Iraq.[24]

♦ Robert Fisk estimates that from March 2003-2008 there have been at least 1141 suicide bombings in Iraq resulting in approximately 13,000 killed and 16,112 injured. Almost all killed or wounded are Iraqi Muslims. Only about 10 out of over 1000 bombers have been identified. Approximately 365 suicide attacks were launched against Iraqi security forces but only 24 US bases were attacked (probably because of high security measures).[25] There has been a rising trend in the use of female suicide bombers in Iraq.[26] Since 2003,

43 women have carried out suicide bombings in Iraq of which nearly 20 have been launched in the past one year.[27]

Suicide Terrorism in Afghanistan/Pakistan/Bangladesh

Afghanistan

♦ Despite Afghanistan's turbulent history and its recent three-decade long conflict, the first recorded suicide attack in Afghanistan did not occur until Sept. 9, 2001 when Ahmad Shah Masoud, leader of the anti-Taliban Northern Alliance was killed by suicide bombers posing as newsmen. The second suicide attack took place almost a year later in 2002, followed by two such attacks in 2003, six in 2004, 27 in 2005, 139 in 2006, 139 in 2007, and 140 till March 2008.[28] Suicide attacks in 2008 have currently shown a sharp increase over figures for previous years.[29]

♦ The U.S. has routinely referred to the "Iraqification" of the Afghan conflict. The current statistics seem to support the notion that suicide bombers are ramping up their attacks in an effort to cause as much Iraqi-style carnage as possible.

♦ Afghan suicide bombers appear to have focused on security forces and coalition forces also within Kabul. In January 2008 multiple suicide bombers attacked the Serena Hotel in the highly guarded capital killed at least 8 including foreigners. In July 2008 suicide car bombers attacked the Indian Embassy in Kabul killing 14 including two senior Indian diplomats and injuring over 100 Afghans. The bomber is suspected to be from the resurgent Afghan/Pakistan Taliban operating from the Federally Administered Tribal Areas (FATA) of Pakistan.

♦ Safe havens for Afghan insurgents are located in Pakistan along the loosely guarded border between Afghanistan and Pakistan. Early attacks were occurring mainly in the southern and eastern provinces at first, but have now spread to other areas. It is now becoming increasing difficult to predict the movement of these groups and take adequate preemptive measures.[30]

♦ The Al Qaeda affiliated trainers reportedly include Chechens and Uzbeks, as well as Yemenis and other Arab nationals.[31] News reports also state that the Taliban would induct almost 2000 suicide bombers from Pakistan into Afghanistan to support the forthcoming spring offensive against the NATO forces in 2009.

Pakistan

♦ Suicide terrorism attacks in Pakistan have increased steeply in the past two years. Suicide bombings in Pakistan include suicide attacks on President Musharraf, foreign workers in Pakistan, Shia targets by Sunni extremists, Pakistani army and police installations and intelligence services headquarters. Suicide bombers have targeted Pakistan with increasing frequency from 2006 onwards.[32]

♦ Suicide attacks in Pakistan intensified after General Musharraf attacked the Islamist Lal Masjid in Islamabad in July 2007, resulting in the deaths of about 50 Islamists who refused to surrender.[33] Pakistani army attacks on Islamist militants in the North West Frontier Province and the FATA against Al Qaeda-backed Pakistani Taliban forces also unleashed a wave of suicide attacks in Pakistani cities like Lahore, Peshawar, Karachi, Rawalpindi and Islamabad.[34]

♦ On October 18, 2007 twin suicide bombers attacked Benazir Bhutto's home coming rally near Karachi killing over 135, and injuring hundreds more. In December 2007 suicide attackers killed Benazir Bhutto in Rawalpindi (near the capital Islamabad) killing 20 others and injuring many more.[35]

♦ On September 20, 2008 a suicide truck bomber belonging to Al Qaeda/ Pakistan Taliban with 600 kilograms of explosives attacked the Marriott Hotel in Islamabad killing over 53 and injuring over 220.[36]

♦ This shows an increasing trend of suicide terrorism amongst radical elements in Pakistan and poses a renewed threat to India. In addition, as covered earlier, Pakistan-based *fidayeen* groups mainly from the *Lakshar e Taiba* and *Jaish e Muhammad* have been carrying out suicide terrorism attacks on targets inside India.[37] Teherik e Taliban Pakistan, Lashkar e Janghvi and Sipah e Sahaba have been conducting suicide terrorism attacks within Pakistan.[38]

♦ The encouragement and acceptance of suicide terrorism in Pakistan as a form of legitimate religious resistance against a democratically elected government could instigate a similar sentiment amongst Indian Muslims in Kashmir and beyond.

Bangladesh

♦ Suicide terrorism has also escalated in Bangladesh. Elements of the Jamaat ul Mujahideen have been reported to be implicated in suicide terrorism since 2005.[39] There is also growing evidence that Islamist cells from Pakistan have established terrorist training camps within Bangladesh. Suicide terrorism has the potential of spilling over into India from Bangladesh, especially in view of the unrest in Northeast India.[40]

Disturbing Trends in Suicide Terrorism

Terrorist Profiles and Methods

Several studies have been conducted to arrive at an accurate psychological profile of the suicide terrorist. Shortly after the 1998 US Embassy bombings in Kenya and Tanzania, the US Government took out a report titled, 'Who Becomes a Terrorist and Why'.[41] Though some progress was made in trying to arrive at a template, it was concluded that it was very difficult to generalise. Suicide terrorists are driven by a sense of purpose, fuelled by a combination of factors to include religion, culture, pride, anger, humiliation, poverty, desperation, lack of education, sense of injustice, and thirst for revenge. Suicide terrorism is a rational act committed voluntarily.[42] It is not the act of a deranged person but part of a well thought out campaign to exact a heavy toll of the enemy. The events of 9/11 proved that even well educated, persons from affluent backgrounds have the motivation to become suicide terrorists.

Unlike most terrorist attacks executed in the past, contemporary suicide terrorists like the September 11 suicide bombers, the 1998 American embassy bombers and the bombers of the USS *Cole* made no demands. No terror organisation or group claimed responsibility for the horrific results. As such, the target country is in a dilemma regarding counter terrorism actions. Since suicide terrorists die during the attack, they cannot be captured or interrogated.

In contrast to the expected suicide terrorist profile, the September 11 suicide bombers were not impoverished, uneducated, desperate youth of HAMAS from the seething Gaza Strip or radical Shiite fighters of the *Hezbollah* in Lebanon. Instead they were educated, mature, affluent persons who had lived, worked and trained for years in Europe and the USA and used the American system to attack it from within. However, there were many similarities with other terrorists fighting in the name of their interpretation of Islam: a thirst for revenge against the USA for its seemingly flawed and pro-Israel policies in West Asia, a devout and fanatical belief in radical Islam, and the willingness and courage to die a violent and suicidal death as a martyr for their belief in a 'just' cause; caring little for their own life or for the lives of others whom they consider enemies and therefore, legitimate targets.[43]

Ariel Merari an Israeli professor who has studied suicide terrorism for years has concluded that psychological profiles of suicide bombers are not possible.[44] This is supported by Nasra Hassan who has interviewed potential Palestinians who were selected for martyrdom missions in the Gaza Strip and West Bank. She however, notes that almost all of them were deeply religious and believed that their act of martyrdom would lead them to Paradise.[45]

In a counterview some researchers have opined that suicide bombers might be characterized by the risk factors that increase the probability of suicide.[46] There is no known typology of a suicide bomber. In the case of *fidayeen* attackers from Pakistan, it makes it all the more difficult for Indian forces to weed out a potential bomber. With the increase in people to people contact between India and Pakistan, the possibility of *fidayeen* from Pakistan posing as genuine visitors to India cannot be ruled out.

Increasing Use of Women Suicide Bombers

In the current Palestinian crisis, increasing use has been made of female suicide bombers. As many as eight women bombers have been launched with success (some as young as 18 years) and 68 have been arrested by the Israelis before they could launch their attacks.[47] In Turkey, out of 18 suicide bombings before the capture of PKK leader Abdullah Ocalan, 15 were carried out by women. In Chechnya the 'Black Widows' have launched sensational suicide bombings in Moscow. They also blew up a Russian airliner in midair killing all on board. The LTTE has used female suicide bombers in many attacks including the one in which Rajiv Gandhi was killed.[48] In Iraq, over 23 females have been used in suicide bombings since 2005 and their use is increasing daily.

The growing number of women involved in suicide terrorism had led to serious concern amongst security analysts.[49] There is a growing sanction by Islamists for women's participation alongside men in jihad. The main reason for women to join the ranks of suicide bombers is to take revenge for male relatives killed by the security forces and also to fight equally by the side of men in a jihad.[50] The use of women cause additional problems for security forces in West/South Asia as explosive belts can be concealed under lose female clothing traditionally worn by women that covers the whole body and sometimes even the full face. A woman can also pretend to be pregnant and carry a much larger explosive pack under her clothes.

In the Indian context, there has been only one known incident of a female suicide bomber named Hafsa, in October 2005 in Kashmir. She blew herself up as an Army convoy came close to her at Avantipura killing five soldiers. (This figure is disputed by the Indian authorities who claim that there were no casualties). Three unexploded grenades were found along with her body parts.[51] In the Indian context, the induction of women as suicide bombers would place an additional burden on the security forces. Female police and military personnel would have to be deployed at important choke points near the Line of Control and other difficult areas to physically screen women. There is also a possibility that men on a suicide mission might dress in conservative female clothes to pass off as women and bypass normal checks. In most oriental cultures, security forces are hesitant to search women. Females are not therefore not usually subjected to the same degree of physical searches as men. As security measures make it more and more difficult for male bombers to reach their targets, the number of female suicide bombers is bound to increase.

Varied Modes of Attack and 'Copy-cat' Syndrome

Suicide terrorists learn from each others successes and failures. They copy each other's bombing techniques and targets preferences for maximum effect. For example, as noted earlier, the October 2000 Al Qaeda suicide bombing of the USS Cole was inspired by LTTE suicide attacks on maritime targets in Sri Lanka. Recently, multiple suicide bombers have been introduced by groups inspired by Al Qaeda like Al Qaeda in the Islamic Maghreb and Al Qaeda in Iraq. In Iraq as many as nine suicide bombers were sent to attack multiple targets in one day. Suicide bombings have also been coordinated to be launched simultaneously at widely dispersed multiple targets for greater psychological effect. This was demonstrated during the 9/11 attacks and the attacks on the American Embassies in Kenya and Tanzania (the Hezbollah had earlier carried out successful simultaneous bombings on US and French targets in Beirut).

Suicide bombers have also used various types of disguises to penetrate security cordons. They have disguised themselves as soldiers and used military vehicles, pretended to be security personnel, used false number plates, and even acted as paramedics or doctors to access hospitals and military facilities. Suicide attacks have been timed to coincide with festive or religious holidays like the of Sabbath, Passover feast, Eid, and Ramadan iftar, when maximum people are shopping, praying or celebrating. Suicide bombers have infiltrated marriage parties, cafes, bus stations, buses and bus stops as well as hitch hiking points used by soldiers and civilians. Terrorist groups are constantly adapting to other suicide groups for greater successes, as such there is no 'signature' or target analysis profiling.

Suicide bombers have also integrated their attacks with other terrorist groups such as Al Qaeda with the Pakistani Taliban; Afghan Taliban with the Pakistani Taliban and Al Qaeda; and *Jaish e Muhammad* with the *Lashkar e Taiba*. In Iraq, many suicide bombers have detonated their explosives at military checkpoints as the soldiers came close to check documents. Suicide bombers have used sea borne attacks, and under water attacks, as well as airborne attacks and even attacks on bicycles and donkeys. Some groups like the LTTE and Palestinian extremists (with little success) have also tried to use hang gliders piloted by suicide bombers.[52] The aim is to get as close as possible to the target and detonate oneself in an area which is full of people.

An explosive device carried by a bomber on his person varies from 3-15 Kilograms of TNT hidden under a coat or a military vest or a bag. Larger quantities of explosives can be carried in a truck or ship and rammed into the target area. The firing device is usually a simple circuit with a detonator. Steel ball bearings and nails are usually added to the TNT to increase the kill area and lethality of the explosion (but this has the disadvantage of detection by metal detectors). Recently, rat poison (known for its anti-coagulant properties) has also been mixed with the explosive suicide charge so that the injured would bleed to death. Attempts are being made to acquire modern explosives for better destructive effect in smaller quantities since vehicles carrying large quantities of explosives are likely to be detected.[53] Suicide terrorists are also looking at ways to manufacture powerful crude bombs in home laboratories from household chemicals and fertilisers.

Suicide Terrorism and use of Weapons of Mass Destruction/ Disruption

With relatively easy access to chemical and biological agents, the threat of suicide terrorists causing mass casualties attacks in crowded enclosed areas like airports, shopping arcades, railway stations, amusement parks, hotels, and political indoor rallies is a real possibility and very difficult to monitor or prevent. Biological agents are especially difficult to detect as they have no smell and can be 'silent' killers.

A suicide terrorist could also set off a radiological dispersal device (dirty bomb) to contaminate a large area and cause panic. Radiological waste and the availability of radioactive material in medical treatment and diagnostic facilities can be fashioned to make a crude radioactive bomb.[54]

Another possibility that has been discussed is one of a sea borne suicide attack in which a berthed merchant big ship laden with chemicals or radioactive material would be rammed by a boat manned by suicide bombers to disperse a chemical or radiological contaminant into the port. Depending on wind and water conditions, the effect of the explosion would be multiplied with far reaching effects.

In Iraq chlorine filled trucks have been exploded by suicide bombers to cause panic, burns and lung damage. The toxic gas so dispersed cannot be stopped by concrete barriers or crash guards. The gas has the potential of spreading with the prevailing wind with adverse effects on a large number of people in a wide ranging area. The suicide terrorist does not need to get close to the target for maximum effect in this case.

Chemical and nuclear plants are also particularly susceptible to aerial suicide attacks. In the Pakistani context, there is still a serious question about the safety and security of Pakistan's nuclear assets and the security of nuclear waste from falling into the hands of knowledgeable extremists. The black market trade of the A.Q. Khan Network and Pakistani rogue scientists' contacts with the Al Qaeda are well documented and will not be repeated here.

Suicide terrorists are always trying to outdo each other by trying to launch spectacular catastrophic attacks on high value targets. India needs to study every major suicide terrorist attack and draw lessons from the success or failure of each incident.

End Notes To Chapter 2

1. For a detailed account of this sect see Bernard Lewis, 'The Assassins: A Radical Sect in Islam', (Wiedenfeld and Nicolson, London, 1967), and Amir Taheri, 'Holy Terror: The Inside Story of Islamic Terrorism,' (Hutchinson Ltd, London, 1987) pp 28-35. The name "Fedayeen" was later adopted by Palestinian guerrillas fighting Israeli occupation in the 1960s and Pakistani terrorist groups in the 1990s. Earlier in the first century A.D., a Jewish group of Zealots also called *sicarii* used a short dagger to kill at close range during their revolt against the Romans.

2. Also see Assassins at <http://en.wikipedia.org/wiki/Hashshashin> for more details of this sect.

3. See Christoph Reuter, 'My Life is a Weapon', (Manas/Princeton University Press, New Delhi, 2005), Chapter 2, *Iran's Suicide Battalions*, pp. 33-51. Over 23,000 young men and boys were killed during just one Iranian bassiji offensive in September 1980. This operation and motivational aspects of the bassiji model and the concept of martyrdom in Iran are very well covered in, Farhad Khorokhavar, 'Suicide Bombers: Allah's New Martyrs,' (Pluto Press, London, 2005) pp70-107. The concept of the ultimate sacrifice for Islam in a jihad was later embraced by the Hezbollah in Lebanon.

4. Quoted in Christoph Reuter, 'My Life is a Weapon', *op cit* p. 49.

5. See '40,000 Suicide Bombers Ready to Strike at UK and American targets', *Sunday Times*, London, April 6, 2006.

6. On 18 April 1983, US embassy in Beirut was bombed killing 17 Americans. On 23 October, 1983 a suicide bomber killed 241 US servicemen at the Marine Barracks in Beirut. 58 French paratroopers were killed in Beirut on the same day at their Military HQ. In Dec 1983, car bombs in US and French Embassies in Kuwait killed 5 people and wounded 86. On 20 September, 1984, 16 persons were killed and the US ambassador was wounded in the bombing of the US Embassy annex in East Beirut. A very good account of the *Hezbollah* and its suicide bombing campaign is given in Robin Wright, 'Sacred Rage: The Crusade of Modern Islam', (Andre Deutsch, London, 1985).

7. Several books have been written on the Hezbollah. For a concise account see Aaron Mannes, 'Profiles in Terror: the Guide to Middle East Terrorist Organisations,' (Rowman and Littlefield Publishers, Oxford, 2005). Also see Shaul Shay, 'Suicide Terrorism in Lebanon,' in 'Countering Suicide Terrorism: An International Conference,' (The International Policy Institute for Counter-terrorism, Herzliya, 2001) pp. 129-133. For suicide terrorism statistics and details see Robert Pape, 'Dying to Win: The Strategic Logic of Suicide Terrorism', (Random House New York, 2005).

8. For a very well researched article, see Dogu Ergil, 'Suicide Terrorism in Turkey: the Workers' Party of Kurdistan,' in 'Countering Suicide Terrorism,' op cit, pp 105-128, and Pape, 'Dying to Win', op cit.

9. See Kurdistan Workers Party at < http://en.wikipedia.org/wiki/ Kurdistan_Workers_Party>.

10. For details of major attacks by the LTTE and photographs, see 'LTTE: A Trail of Atrocities', (Ministry of Foreign Affairs, Sri Lanka, July 2007).

11. For a biographical sketch of the LTTE Leader, see Harinder Baweja Ed, 'Most Wanted: Profiles of Terror', (Roli Books, Delhi, 2002) pp.94-113.

12. See Rohan Gunaratna, 'Suicide terrorism in Sri Lanka and India,' in Countering Suicide terrorism, op cit pp 97-104, Pape, 'Dying to Win,' op cit and R. Ramasubramaniam, 'Suicide Terrorism in Sri Lanka,' (IPCS, New Delhi, 2004).

13. It is almost impossible to list all the works on Al Qaeda. However, see Rohan Gunaratna, 'Inside Al Qaeda: Global Network of Terror,' (Hurst, London, 2002), and Aaaron Mannes, 'Profiles in Terror', *op cit* for initial references on the organisation.

14. 'Riyadh says Al Qaeda Threat not Over,' Jordan Times, April 29, 2007.

15. For more details on Al Qaeda see Abdel Bari Atwan, 'The Secret History of Al-Qaida', (Abacus, London 2006, reprint 2007).

16. For its involvement in the 9/11 attacks see 'The 9/11 Report: The National Commission on the Terrorist Attacks Upon the United States,' (St Martins Press, New York, 2004).

17. Also see Yoram Schweitzer, Sari Goldstein Ferber, 'Al-Qaeda and the Internationalization of Suicide Terrorism,' Jaffee Center for Strategic Studies, Memorandum 78, November 2005.

18. For a detailed research paper on Chechen suicide terrorism see Anne Speckhard and Khapta Ahkmedova, 'The Making of a Martyr: Chechen Suicide Terrorism,' *Studies in Conflict and Terrorism*, No. 29, 2006, pp. 429-492.

19. For another well researched article on the subject see Mark Kramer, 'The Perils of Counterinsurgency: Russia's War in Chechnya,' *International Security,* Vol. 29, No. 3 (Winter 2004/05) pp 5-63.

20. Palestinian terrorist groups have been the subject of extensive research and writings. Some of the books recommended are: Matthew Levitt, 'HAMAS: politics, Charity, and Terrorism in the Service of Jihad', (Yale University Press 2006); Mohammed Hafez, 'Manufacturing Human Bombs: The Making of Palestinian Suicide Bombers', (USIP Press Books, Washington DC, 2006); this publication also has a complete list of all suicide bombings in Israel since 1993; and Shaul Mishal and Avraham Sela, 'The Palestinian

Hamas: Vision, Violence, and Coexistence', (Columbia University Press, 2000). In January 2006, the Palestinians voted HAMAS into power. The government has refused to modify its stand against Israeli occupation and thus faces a major financial crisis. Major international donors have withheld both recognition and aid.

21. Suicide bombings were executed in London, Istanbul, Tunis, Riyadh, Madrid, and Casablanca.

22. 'US general says Chlorine Bombs Mark New Rebel Tactics,' *Jordan Times*, Amman, February 23-24, 2007.

23. For a detailed account see Mohammed M. Hafez, 'Suicide Bombers in Iraq: The Strategy and Ideology of Martyrdom', (USIP Press, Washington DC, 2007).

24. Casualties as high as 118 in one double suicide bombing incident on March 6, 2007 have taken place. Suicide bombings are a daily occurrence in Iraq especially in the capital Baghdad. The surge in sectarian violence took place immediately after the bombing of the holy Shiite al Askari mosque at Samarra which was thought to have been carried out by Al Qaeda in Iraq in February 2006. The US recently inducted 23,000 more troops in what is known as Bush's 'surge policy' to try and stem the violence. Numerous reports have been published about the Iraq war. For casualty figures see <http://icasualties.org/oif/>. Also see Institute of Land Warfare Paper No. 46 W, Robert J. Bunker and John P. Sullivan, 'Suicide Bombings in Operation Iraqi Freedom,' at <http://www.army.mil/professionalwriting/volumes/volume3/april_2005/4_05_3.html>, Ron E. Hasser, 'Fighting Insurgency on Sacred Ground,' The Washington Quarterly, Spring 2006, 29:2 pp.149-166, Beverly Milton-Edwards, 'The Rise of Islamic Insurgency in Iraq,' *The Journal of Conflict Studies*, Summer 2005, pp. 48-70, and George Michael, Joseph Scolnick, 'The Strategic Limits of Suicide Terrorism in Iraq,' *Small Wars and Insurgencies*, Vol. 17 No.2, June 2006, pp.113-125.

25. For the full report see Robert Fisk, 'Five years of Suicide Bombings in Iraq' *The Independent* March 20, 2008 op cit.

26. 'Female Suicide bomber wounds 7 US Troops', *Jordan Times*, November 29, 2007.

27. 'Despair Drives Suicide Attacks by Women', *New York Times,* July 5, 2008.

28. For comprehensive information on Afghanistan see the United Nations Report on 'Suicide Attacks in Afghanistan (2001-2007)', dated 01 September 2007 compiled by the United Nations Assistance Mission to Afghanistan.

29. Figures compiled from RAND publication Volume 4, 2008, 'Counterinsurgency in Afghanistan' and IISS London, 'The Search for Security in Post-Taliban Afghanistan', Adelphi Paper 391, 2007.

30. See 'Counterinsurgency in Afghanistan' RAND *op cit.*

31. Compiled from various sources. See also Khalid Hasan, 'Taliban Suicide Bombings seen as Self-defeating,' Daily Times, March 01, 2007; Waliullah Rahmani 'Combating the Ideology of Suicide Terrorism in Afghanistan, Terrorism Monitor, Vol. 4 Issue 21, Nov 2006; Spray Singh 'Suicide Terrorism in Afghanistan,' IPCS I Post, March-June 2006 at <www.suicideterrorism.org/I-POST-MarJun06.pdf>; Tim Alone, 'Taleban has 2,000 Suicide Bombers Primed for Spring War', at <http://news.scotsman.com/topics.cfm?tid=444&id=186882007>.

32. Also see C. Christine Fair, 'Militant Recruitment in Pakistan: Implications for Al Qaeda and Other Organisations', *Studies in Conflict and Terrorism*, 27:489-504, 2004; 'Suicide blast kills 15 in Court: Quetta Bombing 6th in Past Month' *Jordan Times*, February 18, 2007 ; 'Suicide bombers New Target: Pakistan ', *Indian Express*, March 15, 2007.

33. The figures of those killed are still not certain due to government censorship and vary from 173 to just 50. For a full account of the incident see Lal Masjid at < http://en.wikipedia.org/wiki/Lal_Masjid> and 'Pakistani soldiers storm Mosque at < http://news.bbc.co.uk/2/hi/south_asia/6286500.stm>

34. See for example 'Pakistani Bomb Victims Buried Amongst Violence', Jordan Times, March 13, 2008; 'Suicide Blast Kills Army General in Post-election Pakistan', Jordan Times, February 26, 2008; 'Twin suicide attacks kill scores in Pakistan's Lahore,' Jordan Times, March 12, 2008.

35. 'Suicide Bomber Targets Benazir Rally, 20 Dead', Times of India, December 28, 2007.

36. The Czech Ambassador to Pakistan was amongst those killed. The bomber was thought to have initially targeted the parliament House nearby where newly-elected president Zadora was addressing a full house of Parliament. Heavy security at the Parliament House is thought to have made him shift his attack to the Hotel. The timing chosen for this attack was around 7.30pm when people were in restaurants for afar meal at the end of the fasting for the day during Ramadan. Ironically, The Pakistani government had declared a ceasefire

during Ramadan. Also see, 'Al Qaeda suspected of Marriott bombing,' Jordan Times, September 22, 2008, p.6.

37. See Amir Zia, 'Fighting Suicide Terrorism,' at <http://www.thenews.com.pk/daily_detail.asp?id=42814> and details of suicide terrorism incidents at <www.satp.org> and Amir Mir, 'The True Face of Jehadis: Inside Pakistan's Network of Terror,' (Roli Books, New Delhi, 2006)

38. For a complete list and sketch of the groups see the South Asian Terrorism Portal at <http://www.satp.org/satporgtp/countries/pakistan/terroristoutfits/group_list.htm>.

39. For more about this group see The Bengali Taliban: Jamaat ul Mujahideen at <www.jamestown.org/terrorism/news/article.php?articleid=2374174>.

40. Also see B. Raman, 'Escalation of Jihadi Terrorism in Bangladesh,' South Asia Analysis Group at <http://www.saag.org/%5Cpapers17%5Cpaper1643.html>; Barry Deely, 'Bangladesh Militants Shift Strategy,' ISN Security Watch, December 3, 2005; and Supriya Singh, 'Bangladesh: A New Front for Al Qaeda', at <www.suicideterrorism.org>.

41. Rex A. Hudson and Staff Federal Research Division, 'Who Becomes A Terrorist and Why: The 1999 Government Report on Profiling Terrorists', (The Lyons Press, Connecticut, 1999).

42. Ehud Spinzak, 'Rational Fanatics', Foreign Policy, September/ October, 2000, pp. 66-93.

43. See 'The New Breed of Terrorist', Time September 24, 2001 pp.24-45

44. Ariel Merari, 'The Readiness to Kill and Die', in W. Reich (Ed) 'Origins of Terrorism', (New York, Cambridge University Press), pp. 192-207.

45. Nasra Hassan, 'An Arsenal of Believers: Talking to the Human Bombs', The New Yorker, November 19, 2001, pp. 36-41. In another report noted that over 83% of the bombers are single, and 64% are between the ages of 18-23, the rest being under 30. However in November, 2006, a 57 old grandmother executed a suicide explosion at an Israeli checkpoint killing herself. Also see 'What makes Suicide bombers Tick? at website <http://www.israelinsider.com/channels/security/articles/sec_0049.htm>.

46. David Lester et al., 'Suicide Bombers: Are Psychological Profiles Possible?' Studies in Conflict and Terrorism, 27, 2004 pp. 283-295.

47. Yoram Schweitzer, 'Palestinian Female Suicide Bombers: Reality vs. Myth', chapter in 'Female Suicide Bombers: Dying for Equality?' Jaffe Center for Strategic Studies, August 2006.

48. Arjuna Gunawardena, 'Female Black Tigers: A Different Breed of Cat?' in Yoram Schweitzer, 'Female Suicide Bombers' op cit.

49. See Yoram Schweitzer 'Female Suicide Bombers: Dying for Equality?', Jaffe Center for Strategic Studies Memorandum 84, August 2006; Jabin T. Jacob, 'Female Suicide Bombers: A Political Perspective,' IPCS at <www.ipcs.org>, Barbara Victor, 'An Army of Roses: Inside the World of Palestinian Suicide Bombers,' (Rodale USA, 2003); Karla J. Cunningham, 'Countering Female Terrorism', Studies in Conflict and Terrorism, 30, 2007, pp. 113-129; 'Wafa Idris: the Celebration of the First Female Palestinian Bomber', at <www. Memri.org/ia/IA8402.html>; Debra Zedalis, 'Female Suicide Bombers', (Army War College, publication, June 2004), at <http://www.strategicstudiesinstitute.army.mil/ pdffiles/PUB408.pdf>.

50. See Joel Greenberg, 'Portrait of an Angry Young Arab Woman', New York Times, March 1, 2002 and David Cook, 'Women fighting for Jihad?', Studies in Conflict and Terrorism, 28, 2005, pp. 375-384.

51. 'Kashmir woman suicide attacker', at <http://news.bbc.co.uk/2/hi/south_asia/ 4337412.stm>.

52. However, in March 2007, the LTTE used a light manned aircraft to successfully bomb Colombo military airbase. The plane was secretly smuggled into Sri Lanka in bits and pieces and assembled in Sri Lanka by the LTTE inside Tamil held territory. The aircraft took the authorities by surprise, but caused little damage. The implications in the Indian scenario are obvious.

53. Despite high security measures the bomb-laden truck that destroyed the Marriott Hotel in Islamabad and killing over 58 in September 2008, was carrying 600 kilograms of explosives. The bomber was able to drive freely along the streets of the Pakistani capital for hours near sensitive areas like the Parliament while he searched for a lucrative target without being apprehended (Parliament house, the first choice was too heavily guarded as President Zardari was addressing the parliament).

54. See also Graham Allison, 'Nuclear Terrorism: The Ultimate Preventable Catastrophe', (Times Books, New York, 2006), Micheal Levi, 'On Nuclear Terrorism', (Council on Foreign Relations, New York 2007)

CHAPTER 3

FIDAYEEN ATTACKS IN INDIA

In 1989, the people of Kashmir took their historic stance, and declared it a jihad in the path of Allah **to achieve one of the two honours, either victory or martyrdom.** Jihad missions commenced against the India occupation, and the mujhahidin part emerged as a strike force in the midst of the occupation.

Syed Salahuddin, United Jihad Council in Pakistan[1]

We must fight against the evil trio: **America, Israel and India.** The Israeli-Indian defence pact is clearly aimed at taking care of Pakistan. America will not attack Pakistan directly. It will use India to do its dirty work. America has also declared the legitimate freedom struggle in Kashmir a reign of terror. The need for jihad against India is paramount. **Suicide bombings are the "best form of jihad".**

Hafiz Saeed, Chief of Jamaat ud-Daawa (formerly Lashkar-e-Toiba)

India has been a victim of Suicide Terrorism much before September 11, 2001 and the Kargil Conflict. In May 1991, a female suicide bomber from the Liberation Tigers of Tamil Elam (LTTE) killed former Prime Minister Rajiv Gandhi in South India.[2] In August 1995, a male suicide bomber of the Babbar Khalsa International (BKI) killed Chief Minister Beant Singh of Punjab and 15 others in Chandigarh (Punjab).[3]

Other than the two incidents cited above, suicide attacks against India have been launched exclusively by the Pakistan-based Islamist groups *Lakshar e Taiba* (Army of the Pure) and the *Jaish-e-Muhammad* (Army of the Prophet Muhammad) or their off shoots.[4] These attacks are usually termed *'fidayeen'* attacks[5] (as the Islamists do not like to be associated with the term 'suicide' which is un-Islamic). Suicide attacks against India were initiated by the *Lashkar e Taiba* soon after Pakistan was defeated in the Kargil Conflict of May/July 1999.[6] These attacks increased after the *Jaish e Muhammad* was raised in Pakistan in 2000 after Maula Mazood Azhar was released from an Indian jail as part of the deal reached to end the IC 814 hijack crisis in Kandahar.[7] Militant Islamists based in Pakistan resort to suicide terrorism in India as part of a continuing *Jihad* and a Muslim obligation against 'infidel' India.[8] This ideology of Islamist violence has thrown up new challenges for Indian Security Forces and intelligence agencies.

India has been subjected to approximately 74 suicide attacks to date.[9] (This figure varies slightly from different sources). (Please see Appendix A for details). However, it is not the exact number of suicide attacks that is important but the broad study of the ever increasing phenomenon of suicide terror that is the thrust of this research. The records kept by various security agencies like the Army, Border Security Force, Central Reserve Police Force do not tally. There was no central agency at the Ministry of Home Affairs from where one could access accurate data on fidayeen/suicide attacks. Since most of the fidayeen attacks have taken place in an operational area, access to the site was restricted. Personnel at the Army HQ considered that *fidayeen* attacks did pose any great danger to the Army's security or its personnel. Researchers at the Institute of Conflict Management (ICM) and The Institute of Peace and Conflict Studies (IPCS) in New Delhi have assiduously tracked *fidayeen* attacks since 1999 and regularly publish their findings.[10] The author was able to access some useful data from them. Exact timings of each attack, names or identification of the fidayeen and the details of each attacked were not available for a large number of fidayeen attacks that were recorded.

In the present context, the spectre of Suicide Terrorism is all the more menacing, as religious Islamist fanatics in Pakistan and elsewhere misinterpret Islamic holy texts in a manner so as to incite 'true believers' to offer their bodies as a holy sacrifice in a 'just war' that pits Islam against the 'Rest'. Divine sanction is offered as justification for staging spectacular suicide attacks resulting in mass casualties of 'non-believers' and certain death of the attacker. Sadly, innocent moderate Muslims themselves are more often the sad casualties of Islamist terrorism rather than the targeted "infidels".[11]

Terrorism in Kashmir is a legacy of the Partition of India in 1947 to establish a separate homeland for the Muslims of British India when the subcontinent was granted Independence from British Rule. At the end of the Afghan *jihad* in 1989, the thrust of the Kashmir issue was changed by Pakistan from a separatist movement into a religious proxy war (Jihad).[12] The *Mujahidin* who had ousted the Soviets from Afghanistan were now diverted by Pakistan to fight another jihad against India in Kashmir.[13] An Islamist insurgency campaign was launched in 1989, 'to bleed India by a thousand cuts.' Islamist extremists, mainly from the *Jaish-e-Muhammad* and the *Lakshar-e-Taiba*, resorted to suicide attacks in Jammu and Kashmir and in other parts of India after Pakistani setbacks in the Kargil Conflict in 1999.[14]

The ideology and the motivation of the Pakistani *fidayeen* are based on radical Islamist interpretations of a jihad against an 'infidel' India.[15] Kashmir is just a gateway to the establishment of an Islamic state in the whole of South and South East Asia.[16]

Aims of *Fidayeen* Attacks against India

Some of the aims of the fidayeen attacks are:

- ◆ Establish a pure Islamic State in India and restore the lost Muslim glory through a jihad.[17]

- ◆ Islamicise the Kashmir issue by using the religious factor to motivate *fidayeen* and martyrdom operations to free Kashmir from India.

♦ Internationalise the Kashmir issue.

♦ Cause fear and insecurity in India and abroad by launching *fidayeen* attacks against targets outside Kashmir to include major Indian towns and cities.

♦ Incite militancy amongst Indian Muslims. *Fidayeen* attacks give the impression of true heroic sacrifice. Limited success of *fidayeen* attacks and the media publicity they receive, encourage/subvert other groups to follow suit.

♦ Force the Indian government to withdraw troops from Kashmir in the face of escalating *fidayeen* attacks.

♦ Gain media coverage and psychological advantage by showing how little their life matters, and how dedicated the *fidayeen* are to their cause of liberating Kashmir from Indian "occupation".

♦ Cause fear and confusion in military and civilians areas.

Modus Operandi

An analysis of about 74 *fidayeen* attacks from 1999 to 2008 has brought out that they have been using the following tactics and techniques:

♦ Operate in pairs or in groups of three to four.

♦ Dress in military or Police uniforms, and travel as security personnel on leave in buses and trains. Some also wear the tradition loose civilian Kashmiri clothes under which weapons and explosives can be hidden.

♦ Commandeer security forces transport or use vehicles with government or military markings and fake windshield passes to gain entry into secure installations. This also allows then to travel in relative freedom along the roads in Kashmir.

- Pose as civilian visitors to Public Relations Officers, or as villagers seeking medical treatment at armed forces medical treatment centres normally located just outside the inner security perimeter of most military complexes. This allows them to breach the outer perimeter of military or government complexes.

- Pose as pilgrims or devotees to enter into temples or mosques before taking other pilgrims hostages and forcing troops to react militarily. This tactic is usually used at prayer times or on special festive occasions when crowd control becomes difficult and entry points are increased.

- Establish contact with sympathetic locals to get first hand knowledge of the timings and detailed layout of security fences, gates, and change of guard procedures.

- Attack during early morning, before dawn, or in the middle of the night, especially on dark nights or during festivals when fire crackers are let off. Some attacks have also been launched in broad daylight for maximum psychological effect.

- Carry out indiscriminate firing using AK 47 type of weapons and grenades and 'hole up' in buildings until they are killed by security forces. Sometimes a wounded *fidayeen* who has run out of ammunition feigns death and keeps one armed grenade hidden on the body. As Indian security forces come to inspect the 'dead' body, the *fidayeen* detonates the grenade killing himself and those near him by a 'sacrificial explosion'.

- Try to hide inside a complex after confusion and panic is caused by the initial attack. Lie low in the surrounding bushes until the Quick Reaction Team closes in, or senior officers come onto the scene; then open fire again or blow up one's self with the grenade causing unexpected casualties and more confusion.

♦ Carry out multiple attacks using two or more teams and effect entry from two or more different points to cause maximum confusion and divert the resources of the security forces.

♦ If detected or intercepted en route to the main target, open fire immediately and kill as many as possible before trying to escape or take refuge in a built up area. Then engage the security forces in a prolonged fire-fight to the death. Sometimes, the *fidayeen* knows that he is running out of ammunition and is about to be killed; he then booby-traps his body with an explosive device so that his body blows up when the security forces try to remove it during 'mopping up'.

♦ Attack a previously attacked target for second or third time. This is to show that no target is safe from the *fidayeen* and to test fire opening drills and note weapon locations of the security forces for future *fidayeen* attacks.

♦ There is no firm evidence to prove that the *fidayeen* are drugged or that they are under the influence of narcotics before the attack. They seem to be alert, highly motivated, and innovative, and adapt quickly to thwart the 'quick reaction drills' of the security forces.

♦ If the opportunity presents itself, they do make a getaway, but this is not usually a part of a determined *fidayeen* operation. *Fidayeen* initiate the attack fully conscious of the fact they will be martyred and are usually determined to die after inflicting sufficient damage to the target.

It is worth noting that Pakistani terrorists and foreign terrorists have executed almost all *fidayeen* attacks in India.[18] There are only two recorded incidents where local Kashmiri youths were involved in a suicide *fidayeen* attack. Both were suicide bombings. On April 19, 2000 Afaq Ahmed Shah, a class 12 student local Kashmiri suicide bomber, who was recruited by the *Jaish e Muhammad*, blew himself up while tying to ram his explosive laden car (a Maruti Suzuki car) into the main gate of the Army's HQ 15 Corps in Srinagar. Though the attack caught the Army unaware, it caused little damage. On December 25, 2000, Mohammed Bilal, another 24-year-old Kashmiri youth from Birmingham, UK attacked the same military target by blowing himself up in a stolen car rigged with explosives. *Jaish e Mohammed* (JeM) claimed to have recruited him in the UK. JeM refers to him as Bilal Ahmed. This attack killed nine people including six soldiers. Suicide attacks always draw international media attention and convey the impression that *fidayeen* are successful in their campaign.

In the Indian context, almost all *fidayeen* attacks have been executed against targets within the Indian state of Jammu and Kashmir. The only exceptions are the *fidayeen* bombing of India's Parliament in New Delhi, attack on the Red Fort in Delhi (December 2000), attack on the Akshardham Hindu temple in Gujarat, and the attack on the CRPF HQ in Rampur in Uttar Pradesh in January 2008.[19] One suicide attack was also conducted in Kabul against the Indian Embassy in July 2008.

During some *fidayeen* actions in India, the attacker does not get killed and is able to stay alive. In cases where the attacker manages to escape, he returns to take part in subsequent operations till he is finally killed in another military engagement. Though the rationale for launching a suicide attack is the same (sacrificing one's life in service of Islam while engaging in a *Jihad*), the willingness to escape if not killed, is very much different from the suicide bombing attacks by radical Islamists in the Middle East, where a 'belt bomber' *ensures* that he/she is killed in the self-detonated explosion.[20] It must be emphasised however, that the *fidayeen* have no desire to survive the attack; they volunteer to take part in the mission prepared to die fighting during the fire fight. The fact that one was not killed by the Security Forces in a particular encounter is attributed to 'God's will'. The *fidayeen* is sure that his time to attain 'martyrdom' will come at the opportune moment in another battle and he continues fighting till then.

India's over 150 Muslims are moderate in their beliefs, and except for some militant Kashmiris, have not resorted to terrorism.[21] No Indian has been interred at Guantanamo Bay or implicated in terrorist activities in the Global War on Terror. No Indian was captured in Afghanistan during the US offensive after 9/11. There have been no Indian Muslim suicide bombers.[22] Though some incidents like the events in Godhra and the destruction of the Babri Masjid by Hindu extremists in Ayodhya have affected Hindu-Muslim communal harmony, the Indian Muslim has been loyal and has resisted radical influences.

The *Lashkar e Taiba* has been training *fidayeen* at Umal Basti camp near Muzzarfarbad. They are selected after a three month commando course and a three month sabotage, subversion and surveillance course. One source has quoted that Pakistani terrorist groups get about $7 million a year.[23] There are no monetary benefits given to the *fidayeen* or their families. The data compiled by the Pakistani intelligence on suicide bombers inside Pakistan indicates that the person recruited is often a brainwashed religious-minded militant who is spotted by a jihadi leader who is always on the lookout for potential recruits. Unemployed, uneducated youths are usually located with the help of a cleric in a mosque or a madrasa.[24] The potential bomber is then screened for his motives and the strength of his commitment to jihad. The decision to become a *fidayeen* is usually voluntary.

During his training for the mission, the volunteer is told that his is a temporary life, one that ends with the *shahadat* (martyrdom) that they will achieve by killing *kafir* (infidels). There is no drawing back in such an operation. Spiritual preparation which includes spiritual exercises and recitation of the Holy Koran (especially those verses that dwell upon jihad) help him to overcome the fear of dying and strengthen his resolve for martyrdom operations. A well organized, well funded and professional system within Pakistan backed by the Inter Services Intelligence (ISI) organizes the recruitment, training, indoctrination, infiltration, and preparation of the *fidayeen* before the attack. This also includes the establishment and running of sleeper cells within India.[25]

As per the data gleaned by the ISI on suicide bombers in Pakistan, it was found that out of 20 bombers in the study, 12 were aged 15-25 years, five were aged 25-30, while the remaining were above 30. None of them was even a high school graduate.[26] Most of the bombers were affiliated to sectarian or militant organisations such as Lashkar e Janghnvi, Jaish e Muhammad, Harkat Mujahideen, and Harkat al Jehad al Islami.[27] In May 2005, a fatwa was issued in Lahore by a group of 58 religious scholars from Pakistan that "those committing suicide bombings against Muslims and in places of worship and public congregations would cease to be Muslims as Islam forbids killing of other Muslims". However, the fatwa does not apply to suicide bombings by militant groups in Kashmir or Palestine as "the line of demarcation between terrorist activity and a freedom struggle has to be clearly defined". The scholars further clarified that "those waging jehad and running freedom movements against foreign occupants in places like Palestine, Iraq, Jammu and Kashmir and Afghanistan are beyond its (the fatwa's) scope."[28]

The Fidayeen in their own words

Unlike Palestinian or Hezbollah suicide bombers, Pakistani *fidayeen* do not make 'martyrdom videos' before they go on suicide operations, nor are there posters and banners honouring them in Pakistan. However, some of them leave behind wills with their families which give an insight to their mental make up. One of these wills is reproduced below:-

> My dear father, mother, brothers and sisters, if you really love me, you should bear the news of my martyrdom with courage and be thankful to God. I request my mother and sisters to observe purdah, shun sin, say their prayers and pray to God to accept my martyrdom. I request my father to send my brothers for (military) training and also to educate others about jehad. It is an excellent

path which leads straight to paradise...... I request you again to be thankful to God for my martyrdom. You should know that your son has died the death of a martyr. He did not die while drinking alcohol, watching a movie or television. Rather, he died fighting against the enemies of God, and is alive in Paradise forever. You should not pay heed to those who say that these people (the Lashkar Taiba) get our children killed in Kashmir. You should read the Quran and Hadith and see how God has ordered jehad and what great gifts have been set aside for martyrs.

Last will before *fidayeen* attack by Abu Marsad [29]

The will shows the courage of conviction of his belief in jihad and in God's rewards and his place in Paradise after he was killed in India and attained martyrdom.

Captured or failed *fidayeen* can be a very potent weapon to subvert future suicide attackers. Interrogation reports and statements of wounded *fidayeen* have shown that they felt that they had been duped by false propaganda in Pakistan. One of then said,

"We were told to kill Indians or die. Now that I am here, I see the falsehood of everything that was uttered in the streets of Lahore. When I was recruited all reason escaped me. There was a sum of Rupees 20,000 for each one of us." [30]

Another captured *fidayeen* was able to give details of his training and also method of induction and targets on the Indian side. He was in a party of six and picked up after infiltrating into India by a Pakistani contact person in an Indian 'Tata Sumo'. His companions were detected and killed by the Indian security forces, and he was captured. He stated in his interview:

"The LeT came to my school and took me away. They promised me that if I died, my family would be rich. That death would make me a martyr, a

hero. I was a fidayeen and once I entered India, I had to kill for the sake of the suffering thousands of Kashmir. All that I was taught in Pakistan and POK, all the anti-India rhetoric is clearly out of place. The ISI feeds us a lot of lies and fills us with hate so that we go there and kill without thinking and without reason."[31]

In an interview conducted with Pakistani *fidayeen* in their hideout in Kashmir by Muzamil Jaleel of Indian Express, one of the *fidayeen* is quoted as saying,

"Death in the way of the cause gives meaning to life. We know we are laying down our lives for a holy cause, and we have a firm belief that martyrs will go to heaven. Martyrdom is the real purpose of life of a pious Muslim. We sacrifice our lives so that others may live freely. We choose to give up our today for everybody's tomorrow. The aim of our fight is not just to liberate Kashmir, but to merge it with Pakistan and to create a pure Islamic state, run strictly under Islamic laws. Muslims of the world are one nation, and has to be only one Muslim country."

Another *fidayeen* was quoted as saying,

"Our fight is a Jihad. We have all joined to fight for the cause of Allah. This war is to liberate the believers from the clutches of those who do not believe in Him. We have chosen to sacrifice our lives in His way.' A third fidayeen said, 'I do not know whether my parents will ever know where my grave is, but I will meet them in heaven, God willing. We are in this world as simple travellers- our final destination is the next world where we go for an eternal life. We may not live but we will make the world a better place for others. I have chosen the path of martyrdom- the Koran says that martyrs don't die, they are live in paradise."[32]

It was further elaborated during the same interview that the commanders choose the operating groups and lots are drawn for *fidayeen* missions. The men who are picked for them are considered lucky to be given a chance to die in a jihad against India. Their greatest honour is to be chosen for martyrdom missions. They usually prefer to draw the lots in a mosque so that they may be blessed and successful in their mission. The chosen *fidayeen* take a shower, wear clean clothes, 'shirini' (sweets) is distributed as a celebration and they all pray together. The targets and tasks are given at the last minute by their handler. The porters and guides are then finalised and induction to the target area begins. Some *fidayeen* take on a *nom de guerre* from Islamic history and from the great leaders of Islamic conquests.

Some Examples of *Fidayeen* Attacks in India

Attack on Jammu and Kashmir State Legislature Building in Kashmir.[33]

On October 01, 2001 a truck-borne suicide bomber attacked the State Assembly building in Srinagar killing over 38 civilians/security personnel. Coming so soon after the September 11 attacks, it was a rude shock to the Nation. The attack was conducted as follows:

- ◆ A civilian government Tata Sumo bearing registration number JK 01C-1342 of the Telecommunications Department was hijacked in broad daylight at about 1.45 p.m. by four *fidayeen* wearing the uniform of the Central Reserve Police Force (CRPF). The vehicle was hijacked in Barbarshah area (about 3 Km from the Assembly complex). It was packed with 125 Kg of RDX explosive and driven to the Jammu and Kashmir State Assembly Building.

- ◆ Fifteen minutes later, the vehicle stopped momentarily at the main gate near a busy traffic intersection. Three *fidayeen* got off the vehicle and the driver detonated the vehicle and himself at the front gate killing 14 persons on the spot. In the ensuing confusion, the remaining *fidayeen* entered the heavily guarded compound firing indiscriminately killing several innocent civilians and security personnel.

- The *fidayeen* then made their way through the premises and effected entry into the Assembly Administration complex holding the people inside hostage. They continued firing at the security forces from inside. The building caught fire trapping the hostages inside.

- The fire-fight lasted for over seven hours and ended at around 8pm when all three *fidayeen* were killed. The Army was constrained to use light mortar fire, as the number of *fidayeen* 'holed up' inside the complex was unclear and were putting up dogged resistance. All *fidayeen* were finally killed. Casualties-38 civilians killed and over 80 were injured in the attack.

- The *Jaish e Muhammad* claimed responsibility the next day. The names of the *fidayeen* were given as Wajahat Hussain (from the NWFP in Pakistan) the suicide bomber, Saifullah, Raja Bhai and Ayub Bhai.[34]

Attack on HQ 15 Corps, Srinagar, 1999.[35]

- On November 3, 1999 at about 5.45 p.m. while it was getting dark, three *fidayeen* from the *Lashkar e Taiba* came in a hired minibus and parked the vehicle a few hundred yards from the entrance to the Corps Headquarters in Badami Bagh. As soon as they got down, one of them fired a rifle grenade over the security wall into the military area. In the confusion of the blast and random firing by the security forces inside the complex in all directions, the *fidayeen* scaled the four-foot wall and hid themselves in the bushes inside the complex.

- They continued firing from different directions to cause confusion. From there, the *fidayeen* moved towards the Public Relations Officer (PRO), an unguarded facility just outside the second tier of security. The PRO a major and seven members his unarmed staff was all shot dead. The adjacent building was blown up. The fire fight went on for another 10 hours till 4.30 am the next day when rocket launchers had to be used by the security forces to blow the *fidayeen* to bits. 11 off-duty soldiers were also killed during the fire fight.[36]

Two Attacks on Raghunath and Panjbakhtar Temples in Jammu, 2002.

♦ On 30 March 2002, the Raghunath Temple was attacked by two *fidayeen.* The temple is located in crowded market place and is 150 years old. The terrorists first mingled with the crowd in the market, and then lobbed a grenade inside a parked car, blowing it up. In the confusion, the other *fidayeen* armed with AK 47 and grenades entered the temple killing the guards at the entrance, and continued firing killing four more including a woman at prayer. When he ran out ammunition, and sensing that the security forces were closing in on him, he blew himself up with explosives tied to his waist. Seven persons were killed and 20 injured. The other *fidayeen* was shot dead in the market place.[37]

♦ On 24 November 2002 on another attack on the same temple, three *fidayeen* from the *Lashkar e Toiba* dressed as pilgrims, entered the two holy Temples in Jammu city at about 7 p.m. and opened indiscriminate fire killing 13 devotees at prayer and wounding over 42.[38] Security forces, which had to ensure minimum damage to the holy structure during the operation, finally killed all three *fidayeen* after an exchange of fire lasting a few hours.

Attacks on the Family Lines of the Army and Jammu Railway Station, 2002/2004.

♦ On 14 May 2002, while the Army was fully deployed on the borders for war with Pakistan, women and children of Army personnel were gunned down in the family lines by *fidayeen* wearing military uniform. They travelled in a long-distance bus in military uniform, and entered the lightly guarded family lines at dawn, posing as soldiers who had come from the forward areas on short leave to visit their families. They gunned down over 32 persons in cold blood mainly women and children before being killed by the rear-area security forces.

♦ *Fidayeen* have attacked commuters at Jammu railway station on more than one occasion killing passengers and bystanders using grenades and small arms until eliminated by the police/army. Jammu railway station is the major hub for security forces personnel deployed in Kashmir.

♦ At any one time several hundred soldiers are either being inducted or proceeding on leave from the area. Railway stations in India are large and always crowded with a several long-distance trains arriving or leaving round the clock. Jammu is the major rail-head for all troops entering Kashmir by rail or road and a frequent target for the *fidayeen*.

♦ In January 2004 two attackers from a little known group entered Jammu railway station and open fire. They killed four soldiers, wounded nine others and shot at six civilians before being gunned down. In August 2001, three *Lashkar e Toiba fidayeen* attacked the same railway station killing seven and injuring 24.[39]

Attack on Indian Parliament, 2001[40]

♦ On 13 December 2001, five *fidayeen* of the *Lashkar e Taiba* and the *Jaish e Muhammad*, dressed in civilian clothes and military-type fatigues, armed with AK 47s, grenades and explosives approached Parliament House Main gate at about 11.30 a.m. in an official looking white Ambassador car with authentic looking windshield VIP passes and security clearance stickers. The car was rigged with about 31 Kg of RDX and two of the *fidayeen* had strapped themselves with explosives.[41]

◆   The car was 'waved' through the first security barrier as VIP cars do not like to be stopped and checked. It seemed to have all the right identification stickers and there was nothing suspicious about the vehicle.

◆   Once inside the Parliament complex, the car took a wrong turn towards a high security zone where the Vice President's car was parked. When approached by the guards, they sprayed the area with automatic fire without warning killing civilian workers and security personnel. One *fidayeen* blew himself up at the entrance to the building.

◆   In the confusion, other *fidayeen* spread out in different directions lobbing grenades and firing in all directions. The aim was to rig the House with explosives and kill or take hostage the political leadership of India and as many MPs as possible.

◆   In an operation that lasted a few hours, all *fidayeen* were killed and no real damage was done to Parliament House. All members of parliament were safe and unhurt. However, the fact that suicide terrorism had spread to the very symbol of India's democracy in the heart of the capital was a serious matter.

◆   It seems that the *fidayeen* had intended to barricade themselves inside Parliament House, rig part of the building with explosives, and take the 200 members of parliament inside hostage.[42] In addition to the five terrorists, seven Parliament workers and security personnel were killed and 18 others were injured.

Attack on 10 Infantry Division EME Battalion Area, Tanda-Akhnoor Complex, July 22, 2003.[43]

♦ The Tanda camp is located just off the main Jammu-Poonch Highway. Three *fidayeen* stole or hijacked a military vehicle and headed to the camp entrance. The EME battalion complex is roughly twice the size of a football ground, houses EME workshops and residential quarters and is protected by a 7-ft-high barbed wire fence. Two of the *fidayeen* were in Army combat uniform, which is common in the area while the third was in civilian dress. This is also common when soldiers are returning from leave. Two fidayeen in military uniform approached one of the gates at around 5.30 a.m., when sentry duty was being changed. While their identity was being checked, the militants suddenly opened fire killing one sentry and a JCO. In the confusion, the two *fidayeen* rushed in and the third sneaked in un-noticed. All three were armed with AK-47 rifles, 500 rounds of ammunition, a pistol and six hand grenades. The camp was just getting ready for the morning parades and was seemingly unprepared to tackle the surprise attack.

♦ One of the *fidayeen* was shot dead by the security forces soon after the camp regrouped. The others were still at large and blew up a JCO residential building while firing in all directions. Seven soldiers were killed and nine others were injured before the Quick Reaction Team moved in and killed the other terrorist.

♦ Confusion prevailed about the remaining third attacker. The army cordoned off the entire camp and the compound was searched as best they could despite the thick grass and vegetation. This operation was completed by about 9 a.m. Meanwhile having initially evaded the security forces, the third terrorist crawled along a drain for about 75 metres and hid himself behind a bush close to the main road inside the camp.

- By about 1p.m. senior officers from Northern Command HQ including the Army Commander, Corps HQ and Divisional HQ came to visit the Camp. Suddenly, the third *fidayeen* who had lay hidden for almost seven hours without detection, jumped up from the tall grass and crying out "Allah ho Akbar", lobbed a hand grenade at the group of senior officers. One Brigadier was seriously wounded and died later, while the others suffered minor injuries. Before the *fidayeen* could do more damage, he blew himself up. Luckily the Army commander was not killed. The dangerous incident and injuries to senior officers led to stringent additional security measures being enforced by military units and during the movement of senior Army officers.[44]

Suicide Bombing of the Indian Embassy in Kabul (July 7, 2008)

- The attack took place at around 8.30 am on July 7, 2008. An explosives- rigged Toyota Camry car was rammed into the vehicle of the Indian Defence attaché and the Press attaché as they were entering the Embassy. Both officers were killed in the explosion as were two personnel of the Indo Tibetan Border Police posted at the Embassy. 54 others (mainly Afghans were queuing up for visas to India) were also killed by the suicide bomber. Five Afghan personnel working at the Indonesian Embassy which is located across the street from the Indian Embassy also perished in the blast. 150 other personnel including two Indonesian diplomats were injured. No group claimed responsibility for the attack. The Pakistan/Afghan Taliban and the Pakistani Inter Services Intelligence (ISI) is suspected of masterminding the attack.[45]

- The main Embassy building was saved from structural damage by the huge explosion because the bomber could not get inside the embassy gates and detonated the car bomb outside the entrance. Further the building was saved by blast proof sandbags which were put in place recently. The bomber was indentified as

Hamza Shakoor, aged 22 from Gujranwala District in Pakistan. The bombing was launched to curb the growing influence of India in Afghanistan and diminishing Pakistani control. The loss of its former sphere of influence in Afghanistan has made Pakistan feel insecure and launch suicide attacks to undermine India's relations with Afghanistan. This is a dangerous trend and could make other Indian installation round the Globe vulnerable to suicide bombings by militant Islamist groups.

Brief Analysis

♦ An analysis of suicide attacks show that the *fidayeen* have been targeting security forces camps and are able to enter them with relative ease. They have no feeling of sanctity regarding Hindu holy sites and mandirs, but have avoided directly attacking mosques (though militants have occupied mosques in the past) or Sikh gurudwaras.

♦ There have been no fixed timings for attack, as such one has to be prepared to repulse suicide attacks at all times. In most cases casualties on the Indian side have not been very heavy, though the psychological impact has been high.

♦ Except in a few attacks for example on family lines in Kaluchak Jammu in May 2002, and attacks on mandirs, *fidayeen* have generally avoided attacking women and children. Fortunately, *fidayeen* have not yet used explosive laden trucks or chemical load carriers to carry out suicide attacks.

♦ *Fidayeen* attacks have steadily diminished over the years since 2006. In recent years all *fidayeen* attacks have been launched in Kashmir itself. No recent *fidayeen* attacks have been launched in Delhi or any of the major cities in India. No suicide attacks have taken place using an aircraft.

◆ *Fidayeen* attacks seem to be a very small part of the Islamist insurgency against India rather than a separate concerted suicide terrorism campaign like the one that was launched against Israel or the one being executed in Iraq, Pakistan, and Afghanistan.

Breakdown of *Fidayeen* attacks 1999-July 2008

◆ Approximately 74 *fidayeen* attacks have been launched during 1999-July 2008 (please see Appendix after Chapter 4 showing all 74 attacks as recorded by www.satp.org).

◆ In 1999-**9** attacks, in 2000-**5** attacks, 2001-**10** attacks, 2002-**7**attacks, 2003-**9** attacks, 2004-**13** attacks, 2005-**13** attacks, 2006-**3** attacks, 2007-**3** attacks, 2008-**2** attacks. (see **Table 1 at Appendix**).

◆ The number of attacks peaked in 2004 and 2005 and then decreased sharply from 2006 onwards. (Table 1 at Appendix).

◆ Of the total of 74 attacks, 49 were against military targets/security forces (66.2 per cent), and 25 attacks were on civilian soft targets (33.7 per cent). (**See Table 2 at Appendix).**

◆ Out of the 25 attacks against civilian targets, 12 per cent were against political leaders.

◆ Of the total of 74 attacks, 34 (45.9 per cent) were launched in Srinagar district, 7 were launched in Jammu (9.45 per cent), and 27 in the rest of Jammu and Kashmir (36.4 per cent). Two attacks were launched in Delhi (2.7 per cent) and one attack each was launched in Ayodhya UP; Akshardham Temple, Gujarat; Rampur UP; and Kabul. (See **Tables 3 and 4 at Appendix**).

◆ Other than Srinagar and Jammu the other areas in J&K where suicide attacks took place are Kupwara (4), Baramulla (4), Sopore (3), Doda (2), Rajauri(2). Other villages like Bandipora, Kulgam, Poonch, Kalachote, Natnoos, Rafiabad, Trehgam, Beerwah, had one attack each.

♦ Maximum number of attacks was claimed by the Lakshkar e Taiba, and its splinter groups, Al Mansooria and Al Badr. There is no way of verifying this claim.

End Notes To Chapter 3

1. Quoted in Richard Bonney, 'Jihad: From Quran to bin Laden' op cit p. 343.

2. The LTTE is a terrorist group in Sri Lanka fighting for a separate State for Tamils. It was opposed to Rajiv Gandhi's decision to send Indian troops to Sri Lanka to assist the Sri Lankan government when Rajiv Gandhi was the Indian Prime Minister.

3. This was the fallout of the Indian Government's policy of attacking the holy Golden Temple of the Sikhs in 1984(Operation Blue Star) to disarm militants who had converted it into a fortified complex during the long period of terrorism in Punjab, which erupted in the 1980s. Sikh separatists were demanding the formation of 'Khalistan', and also resorted to acts of international terrorism like the bombing of an Air India aircraft 'Kanishka' in 1985 resulting in all 329 people aboard been killed. India's Prime Minister Indira Gandhi was also assassinated at her residence in October 1984, by her own Sikh bodyguards as a result of the military action against the Golden Temple in Amritsar.

4. Both these Islamist groups are listed as 'Foreign Terrorist Organizations' in the US State Department publication, *Patterns of Global Terrorism*. They both advocate an agenda to liberate Kashmir from India by a Jihad, and establish an Islamic State in the whole of India and beyond. Both groups have used *fidayeen* attacks effectively against both 'hard' and 'soft' targets in India. For details of organisation, ideology, leaders and profile see website <www. satp.org/satporgtp/countries/India/states/jandk/terroist_outfits/> compiled by the Institute for Conflict Management, Delhi. Also see, 'Terrorists attacking soft targets, says Vij,' and 'Valley figures belie Govt, Army claims,' *The Times of India*, October 13, 2003. IDSA publication 'Jihadis in Jammu and Kashmir: A Portrait Gallery', (New Delhi, Sage Publications, 2003) also gives a broad outline of most Islamist groups involved in terrorism.

5. *Fidayeen*- from the Arabic *'fidai'*- one who sacrifices himself for his country or a

cause, thereby attaining martyrdom; from '*fida*', 'redemption'. The Arabic *fedayun* means 'commandos'. All attacks by *fidayeen* are not suicide terrorism attacks but 'high risk missions' where the attacker *might* be killed during the operation though he actively seeks to sacrifice his life to succeed in the operation. In suicide terrorism involving attacks in the Middle East, the assured death of the attacker is an essential part of a successful suicide (self-martyrdom) bombing mission. The word '*fedayeen'* was first used by Hassan-i Sabbah in 1090. Later the Palestinian guerrillas adopted the name as their own, calling themselves 'Fedayeen for Palestine'.

6. Pakistan Army regulars and some *mujhahidin* crossed the Line of Control and infiltrated into India during the winter of early 1999 in the mountainous Kargil region of Jammu and Kashmir. They occupied defensive positions along a wide front on the heights (over 18,000 feet high) overlooking a strategically important road linking eastern and western parts of Kashmir and Ladakh. The intrusions were detected by India in the summer, as the snow began to melt. Costly Indian uphill attacks and strong American pressure on Pakistan forced the Pakistanis to withdraw by July 1999. Indian forces operating in Kashmir against terrorists were diverted for conventional warfare to dislodge the intrusion. This left gaps in the strong counter terrorism 'grid' that had been established, and allowed terrorists to launch bold attacks against multiple targets in India.

7. See cover story 'Deal with Hijackers: Invitation to Terror', *India Today*, January 10, 2000 for a simple and illustrated story of the hijack.

8. See, 'The True Jehad is for Kashmir: Afghanistan was Just Training Ground: Pak Militants,' *The Hindustan Times*, April 2, 2002 and 'Jaish Chief Inspiration for Jehad in Kashmir', *The Hindustan Times*, 03 April 2002 and 'Jihad is not Terrorism,' *The Asian Age*, 14 Nov 2001, p. 13, 'Is Jehad sustainable against India?' *The Hindu*, 14 Jan 2003, p. 16.

9. The data is compiled from Government of India sources, information provided by Dr. Ajai Sahni and Kanchan Lakshman of the Institute for Conflict Management (www.satp.org) and the Programme on Suicide Terrorism at the Institute of Peace and Conflict Studies, New Delhi. The period covered is from 1999 to January 2008.

10. IPCS has a dedicated programme on Suicide Terrorism called 'I Post' and ICM disseminates its findings on the Web at <www.satp.org>. Dr Ajai Sahni and Kanchan Lakshman of the ICM and Suba Chandran and N. Manoharan of IPCS have willingly shared the data with me. Also see 'Suicide Terrorism', IPCS Bulletin Vol. 6, No. 6, 2003 which covers a wide range of articles on *fidayeen* attacks, and suicide terrorism.

11. See National Counterterrorism Center Report April 2006 to April 2008 at <www.stae.gov/s/ct/rls/crt/2005/65353.htm>. Of the 40,000 (approximate) wounded and killed in terrorist attacks worldwide, over 10,000-15,000 victims were Muslims, most of which were in Iraq.

12. Also see, Lt Col. Behram A. Sahukar, 'The Threat of Terrorism and Radical Islam to India', paper presented at a international Seminar on Post Modern Terrorism, September 2003, at The International Institute for Counter Terrorism Policy, Herzliya, Israel and Yoginder Sikand, 'Changing Course of Kashmiri Struggle: from National Liberation to Islamist Jihad,' *Economic and Political Weekly*, January 20, 2001, pp 218-223

13. References on the Kashmir issue are too numerous to list. However, see, 'The Kashmir Question; Retrospect and Prospect', Sumit Ganguly Ed, (special issue on Kashmir), *India Review*, Vol.2, No. 3 July 2003, and Ahmed Rashid, 'The Taliban: Exporting Extremism,' *Foreign Affairs,* November /December 1999 ,where the influence of the Afghan Jihad on Kashmir and beyond is discussed.

14. Some analysts have also noted that the formation of the International Islamic Front by Osama bin Laden in 1998 in Afghanistan, and the inclusion of some radical Pakistani militant groups under this umbrella gave them the necessary impetus to initiate suicide attacks against India. It must be noted however, that Osama bin Laden did not include attacks against India in his initial call for Jihad against Jews and Crusaders, though he has called for collective Islamic armed action in support of the Kashmir and Palestine issues from time to time in other statements. For details of the *Lashkar e Taiba* see Yoginder Sikand, 'Islamist Militancy in Kashmir: The Case of Lashkar i Taiyyeba,' at <http://www.sacw.net/DC/communalism collection/articles-Archive/Sikand 20 Nov 2003.html> and <www.satp.org>. For details about the *Jaish e Mohammed*, see <www.satp.org>, and 'Ready for Jihad-The Josh of the Jaish', *Outlook*, September 25, 2000 pp 31-40. For important facts of all the jihadi groups in Kashmir, see K. Santhanam and IDSA Team, 'Jihadis in Jammu and Kashmir: A Portrait Gallery', Sage Publications, New Delhi, 2003.

15. Jessica Stern, 'Pakistan's Jihad Culture,' *Foreign Affairs*, Volume 79, No. 6, Nov/Dec 2000, pp 115-126 and Stephen Philip Cohen, 'the Jihadist Threat to Pakistan', *The Washington Quarterly*, Summer 2003, 26;3 pp. 7-25.

16. Statements made by Hafeez Mohammad Saeed (Lashkar e Taiba), Maulana Masood Azhar (Jaish e Muhammad) in various media sources. Also see Harinder Baweja Ed., 'Most Wanted: Profiles of Terror,' (Roli Books, New Delhi, 2002). The book contains short biographical sketches of the leaders of above Islamist groups.

17. Also see Sami G. Hajjar, 'Political Violence in Islam: Fundamentalism and Jihad,' *Small Wars and Insurgencies,* Vol 6, No. 3 (Winter 1995), pp 328-356. This explains the radical Islamist ideology behind *fidayeen* attacks as a form of Jihad.

18. As per a 2002 report less than two percent of the *fidayeen* are local Kashmiris. Most of them were Pakistanis or Afghanistan. Also see Sudha Ramachandran, 'Suicide, Just Another way to Fight in Kashmir.', at <www.atimes.com/atimes/printN.html>; Praveen Swami, 'Fidayeen Power' *Frontline,* July 18, 2003, pp. 22-23, and Muzamil Jaleel, 'Martyrdom, the Prize for Taking one's Life', *Indian Express,* October 5, 2001, p.9.

19. See 'J&K Militants Add Suicide Bombers to Arsenal,' *Indian Express,* April 21, 2000, p.5; Zahid Hussain, 'The New Face of Terror', *India Today,* February 26, 2001, pp42-49; and Ghulam Hasnain 'Inside Jihad', *India Today,* October 29, 2001, pp. 44-46.

20. For further comparison and parallels see, 'Mideast Pattern, now in Kashmir', *Christian Science Monitor,* at website < www.csmonitor.com/2002/0606/p01s03-uspo.html>.

21. However, an Indian Muslim terrorist group calling itself the Indian Mujahideen has emerged recently. It claimed responsibility for a series of bomb blasts in Delhi in September 2008.

22. The only exception where an Indian living in England carried out a failed suicide car bombing was in June 2007 at Glasgow airport. Kafeel Ahmed a 27 year Indian Muslim from Bangalore was brought up in Saudi Arabia. He had a PhD in Engineering from the UK. In June he drove a burning Jeep packed with propane gas cylinders into the entrance to Glasgow airport. There were no injuries to anyone, but Kafeel died of burns a few weeks later. The motive or reasoning of the attack is not known. Also see BBC report at <http://news.bbc.co.uk/2/hi/uk_news/scotland/6257194.stm>.

23. Ibid. Also see K. Warikoo, 'Islamist Mercenaries and Terrorism in Kashmir,' *Himalayan and Central Asian Studies,* Vol. 2 No.2, April-June 1998, pp35-57, for a well documented list of training camps and the rise of the Islamist agenda in Kashmir. Government of India, Ministry of Home Affairs undated paper of 2001 for restricted circulation, pp. 22 – 24, lists 27 training camps in Pakistan Occupied Kashmir, and 24 camps in Pakistan / Northern Areas and Afghanistan.

24. Amir Mir, ' The True Face of Jehadis: Inside Pakistan's Network of Terror, (Roli Books, New Delhi, 2006), pp262-268.

25. See a very exhaustive report produced by the Government of India, Ministry of Home

Affairs and Intelligence Agencies titled, 'Pakistan Involvement in Terrorism Against India', 2001/2002, New Delhi. This document is unclassified but meant for restricted circulation. Annexure E pp. 68-143 contains the names of over 200 suicide attackers killed as per the Lashkar e Taiba's mouthpiece Al Daawa from January to December 2001.

26. *Ibid.*

27. *Ibid*

28. Ibid p. 268. The fatwa was meant to reduce the suicide bombings against fellow Pakistanis and foreigners in Pakistan.

29. From the will of a *fidayeen* killed in Kashmir .http://thekashmir.wordpress.com/2006/ 08/31/to-paradise-via-the-jehad-in-kashmir-arun-shourie/

30. See 'Confessions of Captured Fidayeen', December 10, 2003 posted at Pak Tribune Discussion Forum at <http://www.paktribune.com/pforums/posts.php?t=937&start=1>

31. Ibid.

32. See **Muzamil Jaleel,** 'Among the *Fidayeen'.* The author has interviewed *fidayeen* in their camps in Pakistan and stayed with them until they went on *fidayeen* missions inside India. See Website <http://www.motherjones.com/news/update/2004/09/09_406.html>, and Muzamil Jaleel, 'Martyrdom, the prize for taking one's life', *Indian Express,* October 5, 2001. p9.

33. For a map of the attack and photos see, Ramesh Vinayak and Shishir Gupta ' Maulana Masood Azhar: The Ghost of Kandahar Returns', India Today, October 15, 2001, 32-38. Azhar, the Harkat ul Ansar leader was one of three terrorists released by India during the December 1999 IC-814 hijack crisis, See 'Deal With Hijackers,' Cover Story, *India Today,* January 10, 2000 pp. 30-70 and 'The Age of Violence', *Outlook,* January 17, 2000 p. 14-20.

34. 'Pakistan's Involvement in Terrorism against India,' Government of India, New Delhi , 2002. p.25.

35. For photos and map of the attack, see Praveen Swami, 'A Growing Toll', *Frontline,* November 13-26, 1999.

36. See Gaurav Sawant, 'Fidayeen Attacks: A Thorn in the Forces' Side,' at <www. jammu-kashmir-facts.com/fidayen_attacks.htm>.

37. See '*Fidayeen* Strike at Temple in Jammu', *Times of India*, March 31, 2002. 'Nine killed in Suicide attack on Jammu Temple,' *Hindustan Times*, March 31, 2002. 'Militants Storm Raghunath Temple', *The Hindu*, November 25, 2002. 'Pakistan Responsible for Jammu Attack: Advani', *The Hindu*, November 26, 2002. 'Mop up Over, Jammu Tense', *The Times of India*, November 26, 2002.

38. Institute of Peace and Conflict Studies, New Delhi Report of September 2004 on Suicide Terrorism at <http://www.ipcs.org/03-IPOST-Oct04.pdf>

39. Compiled from media reports.

40. For map and photos of the attack see Sayantan Chakravarty, 'Attack on Parliament: The Day India was Targeted', *India Today*, December 24, 2001, pp.22-37.

41. See 'Parliament Attacked,' and 'Intelligence Points to Laskhar, Hizbul,' *The Statesman*, December 14, 2001. 'Suicide Raid Stuns Nation: Gun Battle, Human Bomb at Parliament, Narrow Escape for Vice President,' *Times of India*, 14 Dec 2001. 'Plot was to take MPs Hostage,' *The Asian Age*, 15 December, 2001, 'Top Leaders were terror targets, says Advani', and 'Parliament Attack carried out at the behest of ISI, *The Hindustan Times*, 19 Dec 2001, 'Terror Arrives at Doorstep of Symbol of Democracy, *Hindustan Times*, 24 December, 2001.

42. Four persons were convicted in Delhi for their part in the operation. See '4 Convicted for attack on Parliament House', *The Times of India*, December 17, 2002. One of the *fidayeen* was shot dead during a fight to the death encounter with the BSF in Srinagar in 2003; see 'Parliament Terror King Shot', *Sunday Pioneer*, August 31, 2003.

43. For an artist's depiction of the attack and report see Tariq Bhat, 'Kashmir Attack: Bleeding the Army', and R. Prasannaan, 'General Dilemma', *The Week*, August 3, 2003, pp.32-36.

44. Compiled from media sources including *India Today* and at <www.india-today.com/itoday/20030804/nation.shtml> and The Hindu at www.hinduonnet.com/2003/07/23/stories/2003072306800100.htm

45. For more details of the attack see '2008 Indian Embassy Bombing Kabul' at <http://en.wikipedia.org/wiki/2008_Indian_embassy_bombing_in_Kabul> and Indian media reports/analysis.

CHAPTER 4

ANALYSIS AND RECOMMENDATIONS

Concern about the increasing activities of externally inspired and directed terrorist outfits in the country is justified. Intelligence agencies warn of further violent activities with a possibility of more fidayeen attacks on economic and religious places, targeting vital installations including nuclear establishments and the like.

Prime Minister Manmohan Singh[1]

Analysis

There is no known foolproof method of defeating a determined suicide bomber. Since a suicide bomber has no desire to preserve his life, but actively seeks death, it is very difficult to counter suicide terrorism once the bomber is on his way to the target.

In the Indian context, the threat of suicide terrorism originates from Pakistan-based Islamic extremists and is fuelled by Islamist radicalism. There is no noticeable desire of local Indian Muslims to embrace jihad or martyrdom for the Kashmir cause. In the Indian context, *fidayeen* attacks seem to have lost their momentum. Suicide attacks in India have never reached the intensity of the suicide bombing campaigns in Iraq, Israel, or Iraq.

In India *fidayeen* attacks supplement 'normal' terrorism attacks. *Fidayeen* attacks have been incorporated to add a religious element to the jihad in Kashmir rather than to intimidate the whole of India into withdrawing from Kashmir (though that is the stated aim of the leaders of terrorist groups). However, India cannot afford to neglect the potential for catastrophic *fidayeen* attacks if a determined plan of sustained suicide attacks is launched.

Fidayeen attacks seem to intensify whenever peace initiatives/ confidence building measures are announced or concessions are likely to be made over Kashmir or when US foreign dignitaries are visiting India. Suicide attacks also increase when the Islamist insurgency seems to be losing ground to India's counterinsurgency efforts. For the radicals, a negotiated settlement over Kashmir would mean that their own importance as mujahidin is diminished, and that they would be sidelined by the politicians. For their own survival and pre-eminence, Islamist groups in Pakistan and the Pakistan establishment have to keep terrorist violence alive in Kashmir and supplement it with media-grabbing *fidayeen* attacks.

Fidayeen attacks are supported by an organised well-oiled support infrastructure in Pakistan and within India. It is therefore essential to also target this infrastructure which includes motivation, recruitment, training, financing, operations, intelligence, surveillance, and target selection. Counter infiltration and subversion methods and penetration of the radical groups to root out leaders and centres of incitement must be improved to target the safe havens and the 'jihad factory' in Pakistan.

The current Indian policy to fence all its borders and improve long range surveillance is an important step in the right direction. At the same time, law enforcement agencies must root out sleeper cells and unearth weapons and explosive caches within India that can be used by suicide bombers to sustain their operations. This effort must be dove-tailed with a concerted anti-terrorism drive.

Though a lot of advanced planning and preparatory work is conducted by the terrorist cell before a suicide mission is launched, the mode and timing of the attack and choice of targets can be modified at the last minute by the bomber after he has been launched depending on changing security environment in the target area. There have been very few instances when a suicide bomber has aborted a mission because of cowardice. While it is not practically possible to safeguard every potential target from a suicide attack, certain soft targets will require additional security measures and 'hardening'. These would include nuclear installations, chemical plants and powers stations as well as industrial sites with toxic waste which could be used by suicide terrorists.

Security forces would also have to improve their quick reaction drills and vary their routine to foil target surveillance from suicide terrorist cells. In addition, certain locations will have to be fortified in such a manner so as to withstand a rocket attack. Standby generators and properly sited and protected sentry posts and firing points inside and on the perimeters will ensure adequate offensive reaction capability if *fidayeen* manage to enter a secure installation.

A Suicide bomber is an inexpensive, intelligent, flexible, and mobile weapon, which can inflict psychological damage out of proportion to the physical results. Even if the casualties are minimal, the very fact that a suicide bomber had 'managed to get through' causes a sense of insecurity and helplessness to both the security forces and the public at large. Mental robustness and avoidance of the siege mentality must be ingrained in the troops. While sensible precautions must be taken, the over cautious approach must be avoided at all costs.

Once a successful suicide attack has been delivered successfully, there is no terrorist to take prisoner or interrogate as the attacker is usually dead and his body mangled by the explosion. There are no escape routes to block. Therefore, it is best to pre-empt a *fidayeen* attack in the first place by following the laid down security drills and taking proper security precautions inside and outside the camps and sensitive areas which are likely to be targets of the *fidayeen*.

In Sri Lanka, Israel, and Pakistan the bombers identity could be established from small body parts or pieces clothing left behind after the suicide blast. The cell could then be tracked and eliminated. In the Indian context such linkage is not always feasible. Even though the body is more or less intact in many cases, it is difficult to trace the origins of the bomber as the launch pads and cells are across the LOC in Pakistan. Further India lacks a verifiable database of potential Pakistani *fidayeen*. The joint counterterrorism/anti-terrorism mechanism announced in 2006 by India and Pakistan could go a long way in jointly tracking down the infrastructure of terrorism as suicide terrorism now affects both India and Pakistan.

Islamic radical groups are firm in their conviction that Islam is being wronged and threatened by the economic and military might of the West and its allies. Islamic extremists fully justify their actions including suicide (self-martyrdom) terrorism, as a weapon of legitimate resistance. India too has become a target and is perceived by Islamists as an occupying power in Kashmir and an ally of the US and Israel. The Koran is open to many interpretations, both radical and moderate. Islamist suicide terrorists are dedicated, rational, devout Muslims and are convinced that their acts have divine sanction and that their cause is just.

This mindset is unlikely to change unless the perceived wrongs are corrected. The hard line military approach is bound to fail and breed more suicide bombers if it is not complemented by the political 'carrot'. If genuine attempts to improve and act upon genuine grievances are not implemented, an unending cycle of terrorism and suicide attacks will be assured. This form of martyrdom might even be embraced by moderate Muslims in India. The right mix of military force and political accommodation will take the wind out of a suicide terrorism campaign, and de-motivate volunteers for suicide terrorism, and channel the hate into willing political participation including a negotiated settlement of the demands.

Religious devotion and indoctrination coupled with resentment, hatred and a thirst for revenge fuelled by a sense of desperation and despondency is a dangerous mix to motivate suicide bombers that self-martyrdom is not only the *best* option for attack, but the *only* option that is likely to defeat 'Islam's enemies' in the long term. An understanding of the Islamic militants' Koranic justification of suicide terrorism will assist the international community in developing adequate psychological counter measures and responses to Islamic suicide terrorism directed against it without offending the religious sensibilities of moderate Muslims. Indian Muslims can assist in demonstrating their acceptance of the true teachings and meaning of their great religion of 'submission and peace'.

In the Indian context, the role of prisons, madrasas and mosques for recruitment of *fidayeen* is important. Though India cannot monitor these establishments in Pakistan, Nepal, or Bangladesh, it can monitor those within the country and along the borders. A discreet surveillance plan would ensure that any attempt to radicalize moderate Muslims minds are nipped in the bud and those who incite violence and hatred are arrested, and that moderate Muslims are willingly co-opted in this effort. Moderate Muslims can play an important role in the monitoring process and in all other measures against religious extremism to stem the radicalization process that encourages suicide attacks. However, madrasas can be used positively to teach the true tenets of Islam.

Recent research has shown that many of the present-day Muslim suicide bombers in Europe did not get indoctrinated in madrasas, rather they were radicalized in mosques. They became radical ideologues by negative local influences and unfair anti-Muslim policies that denied them proper jobs, a good education, and a respectable place in society.[2] Suicide bombers breed in an atmosphere of injustice and perceived illegitimate occupation of Muslim lands. A distorted interpretation of religion in mosques and madrasas lends religious justification to suicide terrorism and in their distorted view elevates an act of murder to martyrdom.

The best way to counter suicide terrorism is to pre-empt the launch of the bomber by aggressive actions and very good intelligence networking to locate and destroy the support and operative cells or intercept the suicide bomber well before the intended target. This can be done by an aggressive surveillance policy and a strong intelligence grid. An atmosphere where the Indian Muslim does not feel marginalized and is ensured a safe a happy future in India will keep radical forces at bay.

As the attacks against Iraq, Israel, and the USA have amply demonstrated, no country has yet been able to thwart a determined suicide bomber. The problem is compounded as the bomber does not fear for his life and in fact actively seeks death during the attack to fulfill a perceived religious justification to attain salvation and martyrdom.

Currently the suicide terrorism threat to India is posed mainly from Islamists based in Pakistan. The LTTE and Sikh terrorist groups that had conducted suicide attacks in India in the past do not pose a viable suicide terrorism threat to India in the foreseeable future. The LTTE has not launched any suicide attacks in India since the assassination of Rajiv Gandhi in 1991. (In the ongoing Sri Lankan conflict, the LTTE suicide bombing campaign is nowhere as virulent as it once was). Since the assassination of Beant Singh in 1995, no Sikh group has executed a suicide bombing against India. Despite this, Indian intelligence agencies must continue to monitor threats from all sources especially those organizations which have a history of hostility towards the Indian state.

Most Indian Muslims are moderate in their outlook, and have not been involved in anti-national activities. They are loyal citizens and have achieved the highest positions of office.[3] Any approach to counter suicide terrorism in India must take into consideration the impact such measures will have on the Indian Muslims. Even if a small percentage of India's approximately 150 million Muslims become suicide terrorists, it will translate to thousands in actual numbers. The additional burden of countering home-grown Muslim radicalization on India's security and intelligence forces is not too difficult to imagine.

Attacks by India against Islamic extremists or suicide terrorist groups or against a neighbouring Islamic country (like Pakistan or Bangladesh) should not be construed as an attack against Muslims in general or against the great religion of Islam in particular. India is a strong, secular democracy which values the rule of law and protects the human rights and religious values of its minorities, but its national security come first. However, depending on the severity of the suicide attack, strong retaliatory measures might have to be taken. Being a democratic nation India is vulnerable to suicide terrorism. Political constraints and democratic values may sometimes limit India's responses to terrorism. Some of these limitations are discussed below.

Security Forces Limitations in Countering Suicide Terrorism

♦ Military limitations on strong responses and limited offensive action as a form of deterrence by denial and punishment against a nuclear armed Pakistan. Hot pursuit across International borders to attack safe havens is also limited.

♦ Practical limitations on the use of psychological warfare to refute the religious Islamist legitimacy of martyrdom by using moderate Islamic voices within the country and abroad to influence extremists in Pakistan.

♦ Political and military limitations on the use of military or pre-emptive force. Pakistan is a nuclear power with a professional conventional Army. It has made 'nuclear first use' of part of its military doctrine. The risk of an Indian military response against a terrorist attack must be weighed carefully against nuclear escalation.

♦ Limitations of our foreign policy, strategic ties and counter terrorism cooperation with Israel and US. This might make Indian assets abroad more vulnerable to suicide attacks by international Islamist groups.[4] (One of the reasons the Indian Embassy in Kabul was attacked by a suicide bomber linked to the Taliban was because of India's close ties with Afghanistan and its security forces).

♦ Religious and social limitations in monitoring religious schools (madrasas) and mosques as well Universities and schools that incite suicide terrorism in Pakistan and also within India.

♦ Practical difficulties posed by the difficult terrain in monitoring movement across the border and effective interception of radio traffic. Difficulties in border sealing operations. Problems in smooth operation of surveillance equipment in rugged terrain and in inclement weather conditions.[5] Technology can be 'fooled' and sometimes gives out false signatures.

♦ Political limitations and restrictions on covert actions to eliminate terrorist camps and leadership during peacetime.

♦ Considerable practical difficulty in identification of *fidayeen* from the remains of body parts because of lack of adequate data base of foreign *fidayeen*.

The following drawbacks further hinder offensive and pre-emptive counter suicide terrorism operations:-

♦ The fact that the *fidayeen* support and organisational structures are mostly based in Pakistan.

♦ Limited support structures and safe houses are located inside India.[6] There is some sympathy and local support amongst some Kashmiris for jihad and martyrdom operations against India.

♦ Difficulty in penetrating radical Islamic groups based across the Line of Control.[7]

♦ Difficulty in identifying Pakistani/foreign suicide terrorists from local Indians. Most Pakistanis and Afghans look and dress like the Indians living in the area, and some even speak a similar language. *Fidayeen* are able to merge and mix with locals until they launch the actual attack.

- The shortage of 'sniffer' dogs and their effective working hours to detect belt bombs and explosives further compounds the problem in detecting explosives.[8]

- Insufficient 'inside' information of Pakistani-based *fidayeen* organisations and terrorist suspects. Important inputs like fingerprinting and other biometric data are lacking.

- Lack of effective control over some sections of the porous borders with Pakistan from Kashmir to Gujarat, and over India's Northern and Eastern borders with Nepal, Bhutan, Myanmar and Bangladesh.[9]

- Political restrictions on aggressive trans-border intelligence gathering operations.[10]

- Insufficient pre-emptive intelligence especially reliable human intelligence.

- Underlying resentment and hostility of local population against Indian security forces deployed in Kashmir despite efforts in perception management and developmental efforts like Op *Sadbhavna* to make people appreciate the Army's good work in underdeveloped areas.

- Absence of a dedicated National coordinator on Counter Terrorism at the Central government level (in the National Security Advisory Board) to deal effectively with counter terrorism, coordinate intelligence efforts and operations. Presently the National Security Adviser also looks after terrorism threats in addition to his other major responsibilities. He is unable to devote the time and effort needed to deal solely with terrorism.

- Absence of a dedicated Terrorism Research Centre to keep abreast of the latest incidents/developments of suicide terrorism/

terrorism in the international arena. Currently there is no dedicated research centre to complement academic research with governmental efforts in improving India's responses to suicide terrorism/terrorism and interact with other think tanks on terrorism studies around the globe.

Recommendations

A combination of pre-emptive, preventive, and punitive methods will have to be implemented to thwart suicide *fidayeen* attacks. Some of the aspects that could be considered are enumerated below.

Pre-emptive Methods

♦ Accept the fact that presently in the Indian context suicide terrorism against India is fuelled by Islamic extremism and that all suicide attackers to date have been radical Muslims mostly from Pakistan.

♦ Establish a strong, reliable, and aggressive trans-border intelligence and covert special operations network, to disrupt or destroy the organisation and infrastructure that recruit, indoctrinate, motivate, train, finance and launch *fidayeen* attacks.

♦ Discreetly monitor religious schools and mosques as well as selected universities and schools so that they do not become schools of hate.

♦ Use the media positively to de-motivate extremists and drive home the point that suicide terrorism is detrimental to the cause that they are killing and dying for. Persons indulging in martyrdom attacks are throwing away their life, harming the cause for which they commit these acts, distorting the true teachings of Islam. The media should not glorify the *fidayeen* and make them super-human in the eyes of the public.

♦ Employ the services of respected religious teachers and institutions to refute the religious legitimacy of Islamist martyrdom. Moderate Islamic voices within the country and abroad can play a big role in this.

♦ The declaration supported by 20,000 Indian Muslim scholars and clerics made by the Darul Uloom Madrasa in Deoband in February 2008 that "Islam is a religion of mercy for all humanity. Islam sternly condemns all kinds of oppression, violence and terrorism. It has regarded oppression, mischief, rioting and murder among severest sins and crimes. Islam prohibits killing of innocent people." is a step in the right direction.[11]

♦ Cooperate fully with other like-minded countries in all counter terrorism and anti-terrorism aspects. Despite the failings and failures of the international community in fighting terrorism, we cannot counter the scourge of suicide terrorism without help and support from others.

♦ Ensure that normal counter terrorism and Anti Terrorism measures go hand in hand with a genuine attempt to redress actual or perceived grievances.

♦ Encourage public awareness and participation to notice any abnormal behaviour or clothing worn that does not blend with the locals especially in crowded areas and places of worship.[12] Regulate the entry into crowded places by installing detectors and physical checks. Though this may be resented and resisted at first, soon these methods will gain acceptance.[13]

♦ Ensure good clean and efficient governance and positive affirmation so that there is no fertile ground for recruitment of *fidayeen* from within India. This will also ensure that the culture of martyrdom and suicide terrorism from Pakistan does gain root or public support.

♦ Expand the capability for special searches of females especially those claiming to be pregnant or sick need to be implemented. For this trained female security personnel will have to be deployed.

♦ Institute special identity checks and establishment of a data base of wanted and suspected foreign-based terrorists.

♦ Improve techniques to be able to identify remains of the bomber using DNA and other techniques to try and trace the links to the operative cell for future elimination.

♦ Regulate entry from 'third' countries so that foreign extremists who attempt come into India to recruit home grown suicide terrorists can be apprehended. Passport entry or verifiable identification cards in stages could be implemented even for entry from Nepal and Bhutan.[14]

♦ Implement the National identification card system for all Indians and document all illegal aliens for legal action or deportation. Secure all India's porous borders.

♦ Introduce hand-held explosive detection devices in sensitive forward areas and check points to detect explosives in small quantities that could be used in a *fidayeen* attacks. These could be complemented by the deployment of 'sniffer' dogs.

♦ Keep proper checks on trains and vehicles carrying large quantities of hazardous and explosive material such as chlorine, chemicals carriers especially when they enter into cities or sensitive areas so that these are not diverted or converted into WMD by suicide terrorists.

Preventive Measures

♦ Accept the fact that a determined bomber will get through. Every successful suicide attack must throw up lessons to deter future attacks. Suicide terrorism is a low cost, high visibility form of terrorism which is difficult to prevent.

- Physical protection and layered hardening of important and lucrative targets not only of military significance, but also those of strategic importance such as nuclear power plants, airports, seaports, major computer controlled train control headquarters, water purification plants chemical plants, pharmaceutical installations producing vaccines for communicable diseases. This may include installation of additional day and night surveillance cameras and air defence measures.

- Enhance our current border management capabilities further by inducting real time 'sensor to shooter' advanced technology such as Predator UAV for immediate target engagement of infiltrating terrorists.

- Thorough checking of vehicles including identity papers of military personnel and government vehicles especially near sensitive areas like Government and military headquarters.

- Ensure security of soft targets like military clubs in cantonment areas and open air venues during celebrations like Dusshera, Diwali, and Battle Honours day celebrations. These functions where a large number of civilian and military families gather are particularly vulnerable. Suicide bombers are known to attack during the end of the celebrations when security is lax and people crowd around exits to get home.

- Gradually introduce technical recognition technology of vehicles whereby a unit can recognize from a distance that the vehicle approaching is a genuine military vehicle belonging to a particular unit. This will ensure that *fidayeen* are not able to ram entrances to military installations in stolen military vehicles. Currently this technology is expensive, but over time it would be affordable and well worth the investment.

◆ Introduce double perimeter wire fencing with electronic sensors and early warning devices around all major bases. The space between two fences can be mined with jumping mines or trip flares in ultra sensitive locations to prevent *fidayeen* from infiltrating into the establishment.

◆ Improve defensibility of existing walls and perimeter fencing. The walls should be high enough and embedded with spikes to prevent breaches by *fidayeen*. The walls should also be able to withstand a direct hit by a rocket launcher shell or Rocket propelled grenade.[15]

◆ Fences should be electrified with high voltage even in remote locations to prevent *fidayeen* from cutting the fences to sneak in. Night vision capability and elevated platforms must be manned by night and day to prevent any surprise attack by the *fidayeen*.

Punitive Measures

◆ Since the suicide terrorist has no desire to live, this aspect is the most difficult to execute. Therefore, since it is not possible to punish someone who defies death, one must conduct punitive action against the state or organization that support fidayeen/suicide attacks against India.

◆ Some positive lessons can be learnt from the Russian and Israeli retaliatory campaign that decimated the Chechen and Palestinian leadership and targeted the support structures of suicide bombers.

◆ Emphasize the point that India will never give in to suicide terrorism and that India is a strong secular democracy where people have a voice to redress their grievances democratically.

◆ If necessary India should be prepared to launch a measured punitive action against the terrorist infrastructure and bases in Pakistan as a firm response to any future major *fidayeen* attack.

♦ Preparation for this should be an ongoing process. The attack when and if launched must be swift, silent, proportionate and lethal. It should be based on hard intelligence. Punitive counter measures must make it unsustainable for the terrorist group and the state supporting the suicide attackers to continue backing suicide terrorism.

♦ Employment of Air and Special Forces operations are most effective for such responses. A strong political will and an efficient military will must work jointly to retaliate swiftly when the situation does not allow for any other course of action. Foolhardy and reckless political decisions that have not been thought through should not be initiated unless the desired effect against suicide attacks is assured.

A multifaceted approach to deter suicide terrorism is required. State supported terrorism cannot be totally eliminated altogether. It can only be brought down to manageable limits. Suicide terrorism is particularly difficult to counter. A combination of physical, psychological, moderate religious intervention, economic, military, diplomatic, legal, and international cooperation should bring some positive results in the long term.[16]

The daily suicide bombings in Iraq, and suicide bombings around the world and in India underscores the fact that the phenomenon of suicide terrorism especially one that is backed by a radical Islamic ideology is here to stay till the foreseeable future. Though this form of violence does not meet the moral or theological approval of the vast majority of peace-loving Muslims of the World it must be analyzed and researched dispassionately so that counter measures can be implemented. In any case, self-martyrdom operations will continue to pose a serious threat to India as long as there is internal dissatisfaction, religious motivation and external support for such attacks.

As one radical Islamic leader noted, "Our enemy possesses the most sophisticated weapons in the world and its army is trained to a very high standard; we have nothing to repel killing and thuggery (*sic*) against us except the weapon of Martyrdom. It is easy and costs us only lives. Human bombs cannot be defeated - not even by nuclear bombs."[17]

Suicide terrorism is increasing the world over; India too can expect resurgence in *fidayeen* attacks in Kashmir and beyond and must be prepared to meet this threat.

End Notes to Chapter 4

1. Address to Chief Ministers' Conference September 2006.

2. Peter Bergen and Swati Pandey, 'The Madrassa Scapegoat', *The Washington Quarterly*, 29:2,2006, pp. 117-125.

3. The Vice President of India is a Muslim. Messrs Zakir Hussein, Abdul Kalam and F.A. Ahmed were Muslim Presidents of India. Muslims in India have also headed India's Armed Forces and the Supreme Court.

4. See *International Herald Tribune*, May 14, 2002, David Von Drehle, "Experts fear spread of suicide blasts to America", p 3 (reproduced from the The *Washing ton Post*). 'Police on Alert for suicide squads,' *Times of India*, March 19, 2003. 'Suicide Strike fears put IGI Airport (in Delhi) on High alert', *The Asian Age*, 22 Jan 2004, 'India –Israel-US axis can kill Terror, says Brajesh', *The Times of India*, May 10, 2003.

5. Lately, India has commenced a concerted effort to deploy surveillance devices and fencing of the border to curb infiltration. Despite this, it is estimated that about 2500 militants are already inside Kashmir, and about 3000 are ready to infiltrate every year in the summer when the snows melt in spring and summer.

6. See LeT terrorist Arrested in South Delhi,' *The Times of India*, April 6, 2004, and 'Two LeT terrorists killed in Delhi Encounter,' *The Hindu*, December 15, 2002, and '90 JeM, LeT militants on the prowl in Srinagar', *The Times of India*, September3, 2003.

7. See Lt Gen. Vinay Shankar, 'In Search of Intelligence', *The Asian Age*, 22 Feb 2002, and 'Counter-intelligence set-up fails to deliver', *Hindustan Times*, 23 Jan 2002, 'Intelligence deficit and terrorism,' *The Hindu*, February 4, 2003.

8. 'Shortage of sniffer dogs worries Cops', *The Hindustan Times*, May 16, 2002.

9. The length of India's borders with neighbouring countries is Pakistan-3244km, China-4056km, Bangladesh-4351km, Myanmar-1643km, Nepal-1751km, Bhutan- 700km. Coastline 7600km. Most of the land frontiers are unfenced, porous and allow easy trans border movement. Fencing has been carried out along most of India's border with Pakistan including the Line of Control.

10. 'New Strategies to Counter Suicide Attacks', *The Hindu*, Aug 9, 2002. 'RAW to study risks of hot pursuit', *Hindustan Times*, December 24, 2001.

11. The declaration was made at the India Anti Terrorism Conference held in February 2008 in the Deoband madrasa in Deoband (near Sharanpur).

12. After the London tube suicide bombings in July 2005, big public awareness sign-boards were put up saying, 'If you SEE something — SAY SOMETHING! - Report unattended bags to POLICE -CALL 999'.

13. This is now common practice in Israel and also in Jordan after the November 9, 2005 triple suicide bombings in hotels in Amman.

14. The US recently introduced compulsory passports even for returning Americans coming in from Mexico, and Canada by air. Soon even land entry will be regulated by passports.

15. Also see the suggestions made in E.N. Rammohan, 'Terrorist and Suicide Attacks', *Journal of the USI*, April –June 2004, pp.254-261.

16. The published proceedings of International Seminar on 'Countering Suicide Terrorism' held at International Policy Institute for Counter Terrorism, Herzliya, Israel in February 2000 gives fairly good inputs on suicide terrorism. However, the emphasis is on terrorism in West Asia and the data outdated. An updated Internet version of the whole book is available at <www.ICT.org>.

17. Quoted in Ehud Sprinzak, "Rational Fanatics", *Foreign Policy*, September / October 2000, pp.66-73.

SELECTED BIBLIOGRAPHY

Books

1.   Akbar, M.J., The Shade of Swords: Jihad and the Conflict between Islam and Christianity,' (Roli Books , New Delhi, 2003)

2.   Atwan Abdel Bari, 'The Secret History of Al Qaida', (Abacus, London, 2006)

3.   Barlow, Hugh, 'Dead for Good: Martyrdom and the Rise of the Suicide Bomber', (Paradigm Publishers, 2007)

4.   Baweja Harinder, Ed, 'Most Wanted: Profiles of Terror' (Roli Books, New Delhi, 2002)

5.   Bloom, Mia, 'Dying to Kill: The Allure of Suicide Terror', (Columbia University Press, 2005)

6.   Bonney, Richard, 'Jihad: from Quran to bin Laden', (Palgrave Macmillan, New York, 2004)

7.   Borum, Randy, 'Psychology of Terrorism', (University of S Florida, 2004)

8.   Cooley, John K. 'Unholy Wars: Afghanistan, America and International Terrorism', (Penguin Books, New Delhi, 2000)

9.   Fenech, Louis, E., 'Martyrdom in the Sikh Tradition: Playing the Game of Love', (Oxford University Press, New Delhi, 2000)

10.   Esposito John L., 'The Islamic Threat: Myth or Reality', (Oxford University Press, New York, 1999)

11.   Ganor, Boaz and ICT, 'Countering Suicide Terrorism: An International Conference, (International Policy Institute for Counter Terrorism, Herzilya, 2001, Internet edition 2006)

12.   Hafez, Mohammed M., Manufacturing Human Bombs: Te making of Palestinian Suicide Bombers, (US Institute Press, Washington DC, 2006)

13.   Hafez, Mohammed M., 'Suicide Bombers in Iraq: The Strategy and Ideology of Martyrdom', (US Institute of Peace Press, Washington DC, 2007)

14.   Hiro, Dilip, 'War Without End: The Rise of Islamist Terrorism and Global Response', (Routledge, London, 2000)

15.   Israeli, Raphael, 'Islamikaze: Manifestations of Islamic Martyrology', (Frank Cass, London, 2003)

16.   Juergensmeyer, Mark, 'Terror in the Mind of God', (University of California Press, Berkley, 2000)

17.   Khosrokhavar, Farhad, 'Suicide Bombers: Allah's New Martyrs', Pluto Press, London, 2005)

18.   Lamont-Brown, Raymond, 'Kamikaze: Japan's Suicide Samurai', (Cassell, London, 1997)

19.   Levitt, Matthew, 'HAMAS: Politics, Charity, and Terrorism in the Service of Jihad', (Yale University Press, New Haven, 2006)

20.   Lewis, Bernard, 'Assassins: A Radical Sect in Islam', (Weidenfeld & Nicholson, London, 1967)

21.   Noorani, A.G., 'Islam and Jihad', (Leftword Books, New Delhi, 2000)

22.   'The Muslims of India: A Documentary Record,' (Oxford, New Delhi, 2003)

23.   Mannes Aaron, 'Profiles in Terror: A Guide to Middle East Terrorist Organisations', (Rowman &Littlefield /JINSA, USA, 2004)

24.   Mir, Amir, 'The True Face of Jehadis: Inside Pakistan's Network of Terror', (Roli Books, Delhi, 2006)

25.   Musarraf, Pervez, 'In the Line of Fire: A Memoir', (Simon and Schuster, London, 2006)

26.   Oliver, Anne Marie, and Steinberg, Paul, 'The Road to Martyrs' Square: A Journey into the World of the Suicide Bomber', (Oxford University Press, New York, 2005)

27.   Pape, Robert, 'Dying to Win: the Strategic Logic of Suicide Terrorism', (Random House, New York, 2005)

28.   Pedahzur, Ami, 'Suicide Terrorism', (Polity Press, 2004)

29.   Reuter, Christoph, 'My Life is a Weapon: The Modern History of Suicide Terrorism', (Manas/Princeton University Press, New Delhi, 2005)

30.   Santhanam, K and IDSA Team, 'Jihadis in Jammu and Kashmir: a Portrait Gallery, (Sage Publications, New Delhi, 2003)

31.   Schweitzer, Yoram, (Ed), 'Female Suicide Bombers: Dying for Equality?' (Jaffe Center for Strategic Studies, Memorandum 84, Tel Aviv, 2006)

32.   Shay, Shaul, 'The Shahids: Islam and Suicide Attacks', (Transaction Publishers, London/ ICT, Herzliya, 2004)

33.`———————————'The Endless Jihad: The Mujahidin, The Taliban and Bin Laden', (International Policy Institute for Counter terrorism, 2002)

34.   Taheri, Amir, 'Holy Terror: The Inside Story of Islamic Terrorism', (Hutchinson, London, 1987)

35.   Victor, Barbara, 'An Army of Roses: Inside the World of the Palestinian Women Suicide Bombers', (Rodale, USA, 2003)

Articles

36.   Atran, Scott, 'Genesis and Future of Suicide terrorism', at <ww.interdisciplines.org/terrorism/papers/1>.

37.   Atran, Scott, 'The Moral Logic and Growth of Suicide Terrorism', *The Washington Quarterly*, 29:2, pp.217-147.

38.   Blank, Jonah, 'Kashmir: Fundamentalism Takes Root', *Foreign Affairs*, November /December 1999, pp.37-53.

39.   Brooks, D., 'The Culture of Martyrdom', *The Atlantic Monthly*, 289(6) June 2002.

40.   Chandran, Suba, 'Profiling the Fidayeen Attacks: Suicide and Suicidal Terrorism in Jammu and Kashmir', IPCS Paper n.d.

41.   Cohen, Stephen Philip, 'The Jihadist Threat to Pakistan', *The Washington Quarterly*, 26:3, pp.7-25.

42.   Cook, David, 'Women Fighting in Jihad', *Studies in Conflict and Terrorism,* 28, 2005, pp. 375-384.

43.   Cunningham, Karla, J. 'Countering Female Terrorism', *Studies in Conflict and Terrorism,* 30, 2007, pp. 113-129

44.   Dale, Frederic Stephen, 'Religious Suicide in Islamic Asia', *Journal of Conflict Resolution,* Vol. 32 no.1, March 1988, pp. 37-59.

45.   Euben Roxanne L., Jihad and Political Violence, *Current History,* November 2002, pp. 365-377.

46.   Fair, Christine, C., 'Militant Recruitment in Pakistan', *Studies in Conflict and Terrorism* 27, 2004, pp. 489-504.

47.   Gunaratna, Rohan, 'The LTTE and Suicide Terrorism', *Frontline,* February 3, 2000.

48.   'IPCS Bulletin: Suicide Terrorism' Vol. No. 6 2003.

49.   Jaleel, Muzamil, 'Martyrdom, the prize for taking one's life', *Indian Express,* October 5, 2001.

50.   Lester, David, 'Suicide Bombers: Are Psychological Profiles Possible?' *Studies in Conflict and Terrorism,* 27, 2004, pp.283-295.

51.   Levitt, Matthew, 'In the mind of a Would-be Suicide Bomber', *Washington Institute for Near East policy,* May, 5, 2002

52.   Pak Tribune Forum, 'Confessions of Captured Fidayeen', December 10, 2003 at <http://www.paktribune.com/pforums/posts.php?t=937&start=1>

53.   Rammohan, E.N., 'Terrorist attacks and Suicide Bombers', USI Journal, April –June 2004, pp. 254-261

54.   Sikand, Yoginder, 'Changing course of Kashmiri Struggle: 'From National Liberation to Islamist Jihad?', *Economic and Political Science Weekly,* January 20, 2001, pp. 218-227.

55.   Stern, Jessica, 'Pakistan's Jihad Culture,' *Foreign Affairs,* Volume 79, No. 6, Nov/Dec 2000, pp 115-126

56.   Swami, Praveen, 'Fidayeen Power', *Frontline,* July 18, 2003, pp. 22-23

57.   Winters, Jonah, 'Martyrdom in Jihad at <www.jihadfn.htm>.

Selected Reports and Monographs

58.   Cronin, Audrey Kurth, CRS Report RL32058, 'Terrorists and Suicide Attacks', August 28, 2003.

59.   Gupta, Sonika, and Manoharan, N.,(Ed) 'Suicide Terrorism', Institute of Peace and Conflict Studies, Vol. 6, No.6, 2003.

60.   Government of India, Ministry of Home Affairs, 'Pakistan's Involvement in Terrorism against India', New Delhi, 2002

61.   Hodges, Cyrus, 'The Search for Security in Post-Taliban Afghanistan', Aldelphi paper 391(2007), IISS London.

62.   Hoffman, Bruce, "Holy terror: the Implications of terrorism Motivated by a Religious Imperative, (RAND paper p-7834, 1993).

63.   Hoffman, Bruce, 'Terrorism and WMD: Analysis of Trends and Motivations,' (RAND P8039-1, 1999).

64.   Hudson, Rex et al., 'Who Becomes a Terrorist and Why', US Government Report on profiling terrorists, (Lyons Press Connecticut, 1999).

65.   Jones, Seth, 'Counterinsurgency in Afghanistan', (RAND Volume 4, 2008)

66.   Kean, Thomas, and Hamilton, Lee, H., 'The 9/11 Report, the National Commission on Terrorist Attacks on the United States, (St Martins Press 2004).

67.   Middle East Media Institute, Washington DC, 'Reports on Jihad and (suicide) Terrorism Studies at <www.memri.org>.

68.   Perl, Raphael, CRS Report to Congress, 'Trends in Terrorism 2006', July 21, 2006.

ADDENDUM

Fidayeen Attacks on Mumbai (26-29 November 2008)

Though Mumbai has been the target of terrorist attacks several times in the past, it has never been attacked by *fidayeen* until the night of 26 November 2008. 10 *fidayeen* staged an audacious attack against multiple targets in the South of Mumbai, mainly in the Colaba complex, Metro Cinema/Chowpatty, and Chatrapati Shivaji Station areas. Diversionary bombings in taxi cabs were staged in Ville Parle and Wadi Bunder areas in the north of Mumbai. The attacks commenced at about 9.20 pm on 26 November and were finally terminated in stages by the security forces on the morning of 29 November.

Though no real demands were made, the *fidayeen* targeted foreigners especially Americans, British and Israelis in addition to Indians, and aimed to damage India's economic progress and tourist trade. They also seemed to want a halt to the India-Pakistan peace process, and attack India's strategic partnership with the US, UK and Israel. The *fidayeen* attacks were a combination of hostage barricade situations (Nariman House, Taj Mahal Hotel and Hotel Oberoi Trident) and random shootings (Leopold Cafe, Metro Cinema, and Chatrapati Shivaji Railway Station). The ensuing battle which raged for over 60 hours, left 165 dead and over 304 injured. The dead included over 26 non-Indians.[1]

Amongst the 10 *fidayeen*, nine fought to the death, and only one was captured alive. Investigations and interrogation of the lone surviving *fidayeen* (Amir Kasab a Pakistani national) revealed that the attackers infiltrated into Mumbai by sea commencing their journey on 24 November,

2008 from Karachi in a Pakistani ship named the *Al Husseini*. They then commandeered an Indian fishing vessel the *Kuber* to make the last stage of the journey to Mumbai where they made landfall in the Cuffe Parade area (Badhwar Park). They were trained by the *Lashkar e Taiba* in Pakistan and were ordered to kill indiscriminately as many as they could in India, and die fighting in the true spirit of a 'ghazi'. The *fidayeen* were armed with Kalashnikov automatic rifles, several hundred rounds of ammunition, grenades, 9mm Pistols and improvised explosive devices. They had sufficient rations and toiletries for a long drawn out battle. They were equipped with basic cell phones and advanced satellite phones and global positioning systems. They split up into several groups, were in constant communication with their handlers in Pakistan, who gave the *fidayeen* fighting directions and encouraged them to kill and die.[2] Some reports stated that the fidayeen also had narcotic drugs which enabled them to overcome the fatigue of a sustained long drawn out siege.

Transcripts and interrogation reports made public by India clearly show the involvement of the *Lashkar e Taiba (LeT)* in planning, training, equipping and execution of this multiple-pronged attack.[3] It is not yet clear if there was any collusion of Indian Muslims in the preparation or execution of the attacks. A group calling itself the 'Deccan Mujahidin' claimed responsibility, but this was quickly found to be false. Though the involvement of the Pakistani Inter Services Intelligence (ISI) and the *LeT* is obvious, the collusion of the Pakistani government is not that clear. Under Indian and international pressure, Pakistan took steps to arrest several *LeT* operatives and also raided some *LeT* camps in Pakistan. It also investigated the *Jamat ud Dawa* (political wing) offices.[4]

After the initial confusion (caused in part by firing and explosions in different areas of north and south Mumbai), the situation was somewhat contained initially by the Indian naval commandos, the Army unit based in Mumbai (mainly for aid to civil authority duties like riot control, communal violence, and disaster management assistance) and the Maharashtra Police

Anti Terrorism Squad. The *fidayeen* holed up in the Taj and Trident Hotels were determined to take as many hostages as possible and cause as much destruction as possible. They seemed to know the layout of the Hotels well and were able to booby trap the hall ways, rooms and access to the rest of the hotels.[5]

The National Security Guard (NSG) arrived in Mumbai by air on the morning of 27 November and began to clear the two Hotels (first Trident Hotel and then The Taj Mahal Hotel). Later the Jewish Chabad Centre in Nariman House was assaulted by landing commandos on the roof by helicopter. Unfortunately, the Nariman House Jewish hostages were all killed by the *fidayeen* before they could be rescued by the NSG. A mention must be made of the media-in the absence of an 'on the spot' Government spokesman, media TV channels were the only source for up to date coverage of the unfolding situation. This coverage also helped the *fidayeen* to follow the developments as they happened. Through the Hotel televisions in the rooms that the *fidayeen* were 'holed up', they were able to keep constant track of the security forces operations and plan their own movements. Crowd control and inadequacy of the fire fighting arrangements, as well as the tardy government response in deployment of the NSG has led to wide-spread criticism of the state response.[6]

Several immediate remedial measures were announced which include the formation of a National Investigation Agency (to specifically investigate terrorism-related attacks), amendments to the Unlawful Activities Prevention amendment Bill 2008, and the deployment of the NSG in several 'nodes' at major metropolitan cities (for rapid deployment and reaction capabilities). The police modernization plan is also being given a boost as is the equipping and training of the NSG and Special Forces. The surveillance and interception capability of the Indian Coast Guard and the Navy is also being improved, expanded, and modernized.[7]

Tensions continue to rise between India and Pakistan as a result of Indian allegations of Pakistani-based *LeT* involvement in the Mumbai carnage. The possibility of a limited Indian military strike against Pakistan has not been ruled out completely. However, the danger of escalation, and Pakistani retaliation and its impact on the US-led war against the Taliban in Afghanistan make an Indian military strike unlikely.[8] Continuous diplomatic pressure will by India and the international community will eventually force Pakistan to act against the militants operating from its soil.

It is in Pakistan's own interest to act against militant Islamists, since Pakistan itself is under attack by these elements. The US, UK and other major countries have also urged Pakistan to cooperate fully with India and act against the perpetrators of the Mumbai attacks and to clamp down heavily on the infrastructure of terror in Pakistan.[9] International cooperation and intelligence sharing will also play a big part in thwarting future *fidayeen* attacks against 'soft' targets in India.

The Mumbai attacks have once again proved the danger India faces from determined *fidayeen* suicide attackers who are willing to kill 'non-believers' and sacrifice themselves in pursuance of their militant Islamist cause and ideology. As India's counter terrorism measures (including border surveillance and management) in Jammu and Kashmir, Punjab and Gujarat brought down the levels of violence, and India and Pakistan were on a dialogue for peaceful coexistence, the *fidayeen* were inducted through India's vulnerable coastline. Instead of a suicide bombing in which an attack is over in a flash, the Mumbai *fidayeen* prolonged the agony of Mumbai for over 60 hours and held a thriving cosmopolitan city (and India's commercial capital) of 18 million hostage.[10]

It is estimated that over a third of those killed were Muslims, yet there was no backlash or communal rioting between Hindus and Muslims. Rather, the carnage and common sorrow brought all communities together in a show of solidarity. Though the Indian counter terrorism response to this *fidayeen* attack came under criticism, Indian resilience and solidarity against terrorism came to the forefront with Indian Muslims denouncing the militant Islamist *fidayeen* for their part in killing innocents. Leopold Café re-opened for business within a week, and the Oberoi Hotel and the Taj Mahal were back in business by the end of December 2008. India will have to remain vigilant and act forcefully to preempt future *fidayeen* attacks. As the Mumbai attacks have shown, suicide/suicidal attacks can be executed by a small band of ideological motivated and determined *fidayeen* at a small operating cost with far reaching consequences for the targeted state.

End Notes

1. The Indian government released a Dossier giving details of the attacks and proof of Pakistani involvement. The Dossier titled 'Mumbai Terrorist Attacks (Nov 26-29, 2008)', is in three parts and very detailed. It was acquired by the *Hindu* newspaper and released to the public. It is available on the newspapers website.

2. Dossier released by the Indian Government investigation.

3. Ibid.

4. Several media reports and substantiated by the Indian Dossier report.

5. Also see RAND report on the Mumbai attacks The Lessons of Mumbai Occasional Paper 249, December 2008 and updated January 09, 2009.

6. 'Mumbai attacks call for new Counter-terrorism Strategy,' *The Economic Times*, January 12, 2009.

7. See 'Balloon Mounted Radars from Israel to help Navy Monitor Coastline', *Indian Express* (on line), January 20, 2009.

8. Pranab rules out Israeli-type action against Pakistan, at http://www.thehindu.com/2009/01/11/stories/2009011154330800.htm

9. See K Alan Kronstadt, 'Terrorist attack in Mumbai, India and Implications for US Interests', Congressional Research Service, December 19, 2008.

10. Also see Stratfor report 'Strategic Motivations for Mumbai Attacks' at http://www.stratfor.com/weekly/20081201_strategic_motivations_mumbai_attack

APPENDIX

DATA ON FIDAYEEN ATTACKS (1999-2007)

(Refers to Chapter 3)

Suicide attacks in 2007	
June 1 2007	Two soldiers died and 16 others inured in an encounter with two suicide squad (Fidayeen) cadres of the LeT follwing their attack on the Army convoy as well as STC of the J&K Police at Sheeri in the Baramulla district. Both the terrorists were also killed in the gun-battle. LeT spokesman, Abdullah Ghaznavi, claimed that the incident at Sheeri was his group's Fidayeen attack. He claimed that five police personnel and six soldiers of the army were killed and 15 more injured and confirmed that both the suicide squad cadres were killed in the operation.
July 26 2007	In a Fidayeen attack, SFs killed both the militants at an encampment on the premises of Bhaba Atomic Research Centre at Zakoora on the outskirts of capital Srinagar. Director General of Police, Kuldeep Khoda, informed that two LeT militants made an unsuccessful attempt to sneak into a formation of the paramilitary Central Reserve Police Force at the defunct BARC facility at Zakoora. Both the militants, who emerged from a deserted orchard, lobbed hand grenades and opened gunfire on the pillboxes in the rear of the camp. Even as eight soldiers sustained injuries, the troops shot dead both the militants and also recovered two AK-56 rifles and three hand grenades from their possession. He said that one of the slain militants was identified as Feroz Ahmed Khan, a resident of Kangan in the Kashmir valley, and another was believed to be a Pakistani national. A LeT spokesman, Abdullah Ghaznavi claimed responsibility of the two-and-a-half-hour-long attacks and reportedly identified the slain militants as Feroz Khan alias Abu Muslim and a "guest militant" Abu Ma'az.
October 11-12 2007	Two suicide bombers were killed and three paramilitary personnel wounded in a suicide attack on a CRPF camp near the Dal Lake in capital Srinagar. The two heavily armed suicide militants entered into the makeshift battalion headquarters of the CRPF on October 11. Police and CRPF personnel on October 12 killed the two suicide bombers. The spokesman of the LeT, Abdullah Ghaznavi, in a satellite telephonic conversation from Pakistan claimed that a suicide squad from his group had stormed the camp.

Suicide attacks in 2006	
April22, 2006	An explosive laden car driven by a suspected Fidayeen (suicide squad) terrorist blew up ahead of few kilometers from the intended target of an Indian Air Force base in Awantipura. The unidentified suicide attacker is killed while there were no other casualties.
May 23, 2006	A few hours ahead of Prime Minister Manmohan Singh's visit to the Kashmir Valley to convene a roundtable conference in the capital Srinagar, a suicide bomber blew himself up as a patrol party of the Border Security Force (BSF) passed Hyderpora colony, just a couple of kilometers away from Srinagar Airport injuring at least 25 BSF personnel. The suicide bomber triggered an explosive laden car near Hyderpora airport road and besides killing himself, also injured at least 25 BSF personnel. The Hizb-ul-Mujahideen (HM) claimed responsibility for the attack.
October 5, 2006	With 10 fatalities - five Jammu and Kashmir Police (JKP) personnel, two Central Reserve Police Force (CRPF) soldiers, two terrorists and one civilian - the overnight gun-battle between the holed up terrorists and security forces in the business hub of Budshah Chowk in capital Srinagar ended in the afternoon. Approximately 30 people sustained injuries in the suicide attack. Director General of JKP, Gopal Sharma, said that the 27-hour-long operation ended with the toll of 10 human lives after both of the Fidayeen (suicide squad), who occupied the second floor of New Standard Hotel for about 20 hours, were shot dead by Police and CRPF. Spokesman of the Al-Mansoorian outfit, Aamir Mir, identified the two terrorists killed as Tariq Ahmed Bhat and Mohammad Mushtaq.
Suicide Attacks 2005	
November 14 2005	Two soldiers of the Central Reserve Police Force (CRPF) and an equal number of civilians are killed while 17 persons, including a Japanese journalist, sustain injuries when terrorists carried out a Fidayeen attack at the business hub of Lalchowk in the capital city of Srinagar. After six hours of the cordon-and-search operation, Police managed to rescue as many as 70 civilians. The Al-Mansooran has taken responsibility for the attack.

Date	Target	Casualties
November 23, 2005	Central Reserve Police Force (CRPF) company headquarters, Srinagar	In a Fidayeen (suicide squad) attack at Hawal on the outskirts of capital Srinagar, two terrorists and three CRPF personnel are killed while seven persons are wounded when the former storm a CRPF company headquarters of the 96th battalion housed at the defunct Firdos Cinema Hall. The heavily-armed terrorists are killed 15 minutes after they launched the attack.
November 2, 2005	Old residence of the outgoing Chief Minister, Mufti Mohammad Sayeed, Srinagar	At least 10 persons including a 10-year-old boy, a female pedestrian, three police personnel and the terrorist himself are killed and 18 persons are wounded in a Fidayeen attack, when a JeM terrorist detonates a powerful car bomb in the Nowgam area of Srinagar near the old residence of Mufti Mohammad Sayeed, a few hours before the swearing in of Ghulam Nabi Azad as the tenth Chief Minister of Jammu and Kashmir.
October 15 2005	J&K Education Minister Killed in Srinagar	2 fidayeen in police uniform Al Mansooran claimed responsibility. One Fidayeen escaped one killed.
October 7, 2005	State Bank of India Sopore Baramulla Distt	Troops foil a suicide squad attack on a BSF camp at the State Bank of India Sopore Baramulla dist. 2 Fidayeen killed 10 soldiers injured 1 Killed.
July 29, 2005	Budshah Chowk Srinagar	In an attack at in the heart of the capital city of Srinagar, terrorists kill two security force (SF) personnel and injure at least 18 civilians, including ten journalists, and four SF personnel. The Al-Mansooran outfit has claimed responsibility for the 'suicide attack'. The Jamiat-ul-Mujahideen and J&K Islamic Front have also made separate claims.

July 20 ,2005	Army convoy, Srinagar	A Major of the Indian Army and two soldiers are among five people killed and 17 persons are wounded when a suspected suicide bomber rams an explosive-laden car into an Army vehicle.
July 15, 2 0 0 5	Ayodhya Temple	6 fidayeen try to infiltrate into the Ram Janam Bhoomi complex and destroy th Temple. All 6 are killed No other injuries.
J u n e 1 9 , 2005	Commando Group and Sub-Divisional Police Office in the Mendhar town of Poonch district.	Two suicide squad terrorists and a civilian are killed while three police personnel sustain injuries when the latter repulsed a terrorist attack
April 6, 2005	Tourist Reception Centre, Srinagar	A day before the bus from Srinagar to Muzaffarabad in Pakistan occupied Kashmir is to be flagged off, two Fidayeen terrorists attacked the Tourist Reception Centre which was reportedly accommodating 24 passengers. Both the terrorists were killed in the ensuing gun-battle and seven persons, including a police personnel, were injured.
M a r c h 3 0 ,2005	Border Security Force post, Arampora	Two terrorists and a paramilitary soldier were killed when a group of two Fidayeen terrorists attempted to storm a BSF post at Arampora in the Sopore town of Baramulla district.
Februa- ry 2 4 , 2005	D i v i s i o n a l Commissioner's office, Srinagar	Three police personnel, a woman employee of the Revenue Department and two terrorists are killed and four persons sustain injuries during a Fidayeen attack at the Divisional Commissioner's office in the capital Srinagar.
Januar- y 7, 2005	Income Tax office, Srinagar	A Deputy Commandant of the BSF, two soldiers, one police personnel and a civilian are killed and four persons sustain injuries when a two-member Fidayeen attacked the Income Tax office in Srinagar. While one of the terrorists was killed on January 7, the other was shot dead the next day.

SUICIDE ATTACKS IN 2004		
December 3, 2004	SOG camp, Sopore	Fidayeen terrorists attack a Central Reserve Police Force (CRPF) guarded SOG camp in Sopore, Baramulla district, killing five CRPF personnel and wounding two others. Two terrorists were also killed in the attack.
November 17, 2004	Shere-Kashmir International Cricket Stadium, Srinagar	Security forces killed two Fidayeen terrorists near the Shere-Kashmir International Cricket Stadium in Sonwar Bagh, Srinagar, the venue of Prime Minister Manmohan Singh's public meeting.
October 9, 2004	Army convoy	In a suicide attack on an army convoy, at least four soldiers and a civilian driver were killed while 35 others sustained injuries near Harrath bridge, Singhpura on the Srinagar-Baramulla highway.
September 12, 2004	Central Reserve Police Force (CRPF) camp, Srinagar	The overnight suicide attack on a paramilitary formation at Dalgate in the capital city of Srinagar ended on September 12 with the death of two Deputy Commandants of the CRPF. Both the suicide squad terrorists were killed by the security forces.
September 24, 2004	Akshram dham Temple Gandhagar	2 fidayeen the Temple and opened fire killing 29 pilgrims. Long gun battle
August 4, 2004	CRPF camp, Srinagar	Nine CRPF personnel, including a company commander, and one terrorist are killed and nine people sustain injuries during an encounter after two terrorists stormed a CRPF camp in the Rajbagh bcally of capital Srinagar.
July 28, 2004	CRPF camp, Srinagar	Five CRPF personnel and two terrorists were killed during an overnight gun-battle inside the para-military force camp on the banks of Dal Lake in Srinagar.
April 25, 2004	Chief Minister's daughter and People's Democratic Party (PDP) chief, Mehbooba Mufti	In the second terrorist attack on Mehbooba Mufti, at least three persons are killed and 30 sustain injuries during an election rally at Khull Ahmedabad in the Kulgam district.

April 23 2004,	Congress party headquarters, Srinagar	10 persons are wounded in a terrorist attack on the Congress headquarters in Srinagar.
April 8 , 2004	Election rally of the ruling PDP	At least 11 persons are killed and 58 others are wounded during a terrorist attack on an election rally of the PDP in the border town of Uri in Baramula district. Among those injured are Finance Minister Muzaffar Hussain Baig and Housing Minister Ghulam Hassan Mir.
March 9, 2004	Press Enclave, Srinagar	Offices of the Press Information Bureau and Directorate of Information of the Government of Jammu and Kashmir are destroyed during a fire even as troops kill two suicide squad terrorists who attacked and occupied the three-storeyed building in the Press Enclave area.
March 3, 2004	District Jail, Jammu	Seven persons, including four police personnel and two under-trial terrorists, are killed and six persons sustain injuries when a lone suicide terrorist attacked a police bus carrying 13 under-trials, mostly terrorists, from the district jail to the Court complex in Jammu.
January 2, 2004	Jammu Railway Station	Two Fidayeen (suicide squad) terrorists attack the Jammu Railway Station killing four soldiers and injuring nine others and six civilians.
Suicide Attacks 2003		
November 18, 2003	15 Corps Headquarters at Indira Nagar in the capital Srinagar.	One soldier is killed and two others are injured when two Fidayeen terrorists launched an attack outside the Army's 15 Corps Headquarters.
October 17, 2003	Official residence of Chief Minister Mufti Mohammad Sayeed on Maulana Azad Road in capital Srinagar.	Security forces foil the first Fidayeen attack on the official residence. Both the terrorists and two BSF personnel are killed while ten persons, including three photojournalists, sustain injuries.
September 4, 2003	Security force camp in Poonch town.	Security forces foil a Fidayeen attack killing two foreign mercenaries. A woman is killed while three persons, including two infants, are injured in terrorist firing.

July 22, 2003	Army camp at village Bangti on the Tanda road in Akhnoor, Jammu.	A three-member fidayeen (suicide squad) storms an army camp killing eight SF personnel, including a Brigadier, and injuring 12 others, including four top Generals, a Brigadier and two Colonels.
June 28, 2003	Army installation at the Dogra Regiment camp in Sunjwan on the outskirts of Jammu city.	In the first major terrorist strike since Prime Minister Vajpayee's April 18-peace initiative, two fidayeen (suicide squad) terrorists attack an army installation killing 12 soldiers and injuring seven others, including a Lieutenant, before being killed by the troops.
May 15, 2003	Army unit in Poonch town.	A suicide terrorist in police uniform carries out an attack outside an army unit in the Poonch town killing one security force personnel before escaping from the spot. He was later killed during an encounter near the Betar nullah the next day.
April 26, 2003	Local station of the All India Radio in Srinagar.	A group of fidayeen attacks the local station of AIR. Three terrorists and two SF personnel are killed and eight others injured in the ensuing encounter.
April 25, 2003	Sector-11 headquarters of the Border Security Force at Madar in the Bandipore area of Baramulla district.	Two unidentified terrorists conduct a suicide attack killing three BSF personnel. Later, both the terrorists and a civilian are killed in retaliatory firing. Four more BSF personnel and three civilians sustain injuries in the attack.
March 14 2003,	Poonch Bus Stand, Poonch district.	Three civilians and a Deputy Superintendent of Police are killed in a fidayeen (suicide squad) attack on a Muharram procession.

Suicide Attacks in 2002

December 19 ,2002	Army post in Khablan village, Thanamandi area, Rajouri district.	A Lashkar-e-Toiba suicide terrorist and one SF personnel are killed while three more SF personnel are injured in a suicide attack.
November 24 , 2002	Raghunath and Panjbakhtar temples, Jammu	13 persons, including three fidayeen, killed.
November 22 , 2002	CRPF camp, Srinagar	Six SF personnel killed.
May 29 , 2002	District Police Lines, Doda	Three SF personnel killed.
May 14 , 2002	Three fidayeen attack Kaluchak cantonment in Jammu.	36 persons, including SF personnel, their family members and civilians, killed; 48 injured.
March 30 , 2002	Two fidayeen attack Raghunath temple in Jammu.	Three SF personnel killed and 20 injured. Both fidayeen killed in retaliatory action.
March 29 , 2002	A group of three fidayeen (suicide) terrorists attack a Border Security Force (BSF) camp at Kalakote.	Two SF personnel killed and another inured.

Suicide Attacks in 2001

December 13, 2001	Parliament House new Delhi	5 fidayeen of LeT and Je M. in Civilian clothes. Used official looking Ambassador to gain entry. 2 had explosives belts. All fidayeen killed.
December 4, 2001	A three-member fidayeen (suicide) squad, of the Lashkar-e-Toiba (LeT) attacked a SF camp at Handwara, Kupwara.	Two SF personnel killed. Two SF personnel and two civilians injured. Three fidayeen killed in retaliatory action.

Novem-ber 17, 2001	Three terrorists attack a security force (SF) base at Ramban, Doda.	10 SF personnel and four civilians killed.
October 1, 2001	Four Jaish-e-Mohammed (JeM) suicide terrorists, fidayeen, attack the State Legislature Complex in Srinagar.	11 SF personnel and 24 civilians killed. Four fidayeen killed in retaliatory action.
September 17, 2001	SF personnel sleeping inside the basement of a building in Handwara, Kupwara, attacked by two fidayeen of the LeT using grenades. One fidayeen was killed by SF personnel in the building while the other escaped after the attack.	Nine SF personnel killed. One fidayeen killed in retaliatory action.
August 23, 2001	Six terrorists attack Poonch police station	Seven killed
July 15, 2001	Lashkar terrorists attack base at Shahlal, Kupwara.	Five killed, eight others injured
April 14, 2001	Fidayeen attack on Army base at Lassipora, Kupwara.	Six personnel killed
March 26, 2001	Fidayeen attack on CRPF base at Wazir Bagh in Srinagar	Four personnel killed
February 9, 2001	Fidayeen squad drawn from LeT and Al Umar Mujahideen attack police control room in Srinagar	Eight personnel killed

SUICIDE ATTACKS 2000

December 25, 2000	Second human bomb attack targeting Army Head Quarters at Badami Bagh in Srinagar.	Four personnel killed
December 22 ,2000	A Lashkar-e-Toiba (LeT) fidayeen squad launches an attack within the army garrison at Red Fort in New Delhi. All members of the squad escape after the attack.	Three personnel killed
December 16 , 2000	Fidayeen attack on a camp at Mendhar in Rajouri district, the two attackers manage to escape after the attack.	Two personnel killed
April 19 , 2000	First human bomb attack targeting Army Head Quarters at Badami Bagh in Srinagar.	Two personnel
January 7 ,2000	Metrological Centre, Srinagar fidayeen attack	Four personnel

SUICIDE ATTACKS 1999		
December 27, 1999	Special Operations Group HQ, Srinagar	One DSP, 11 personnel
December 15 , 1999	Civil Lines area, Srinagar	Five personnel
December 2 ,1999	Army HQ, Baramulla	One JCO
November 3 ,1999	Army Corps Headquarters, Badamibagh, Srinagar	10 personnel, including Defence Public Relations Officer
August 13 ,1999	Army camp, Beerwah	Three personnel
August 7 ,1999	Army camp, Trehgam	Colonel, three personnel
August 6 ,1999	Army camp, Natnoos	Major, two JCOs
July 1 3 ,1999	BSF camp, Bandipora	DIG & four personnel

TABLE 1: FIDAYEEN ATTACKS BY YEAR

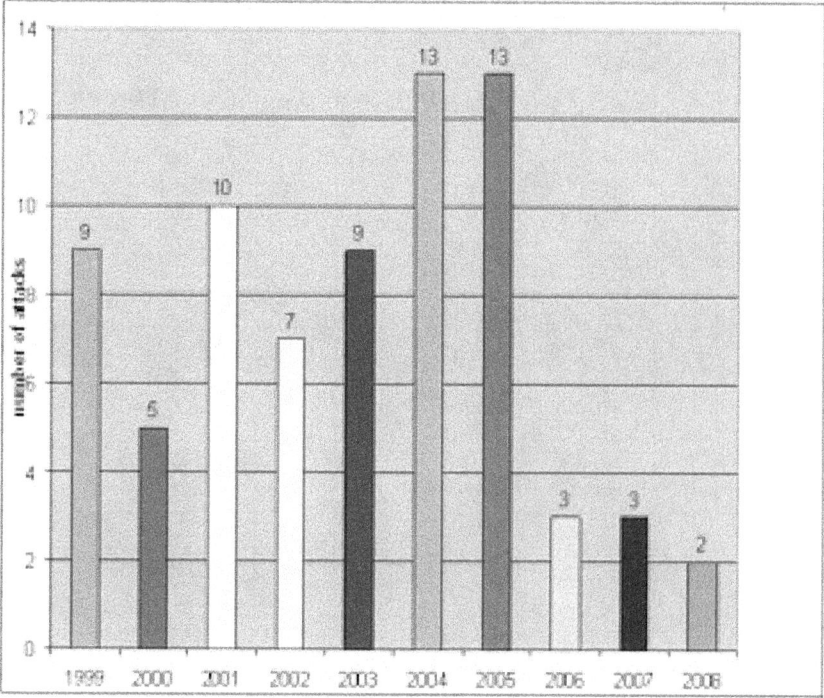

TABLE 2: ATTACKS ON CIVILIAN AND MILITARY TARGETS

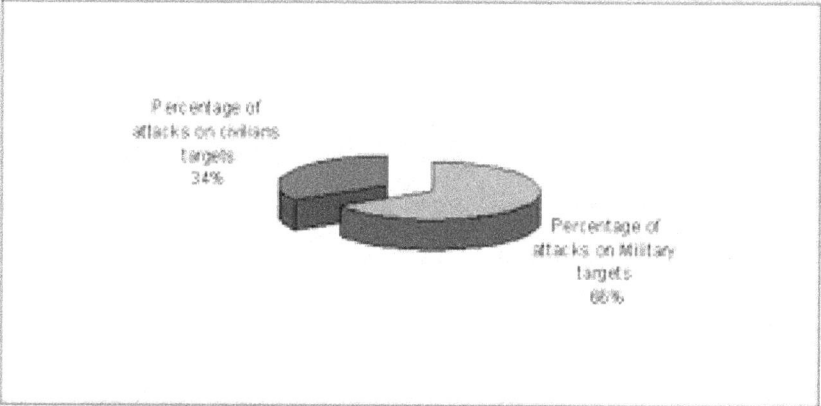

Appendix -reference Chapter 3 page 13

TABLE 3 : AREA-WISE BREAKDOWN OF NUMBER OF ATTACKS

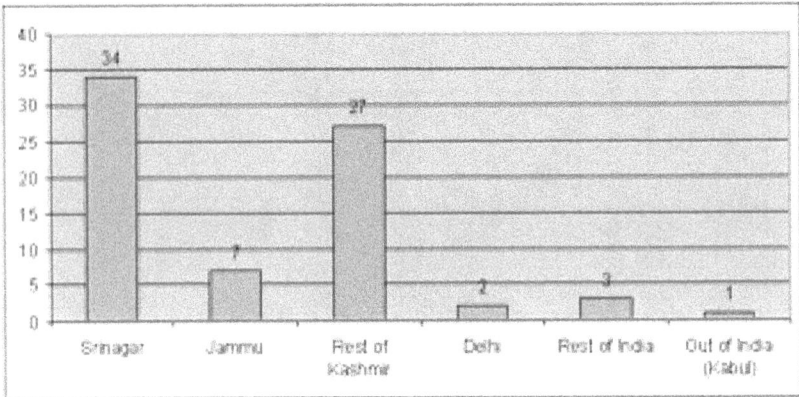

TABLE 4 : AREA-WISE BREAKDOWN OF PERCENTAGE OF ATTACKS

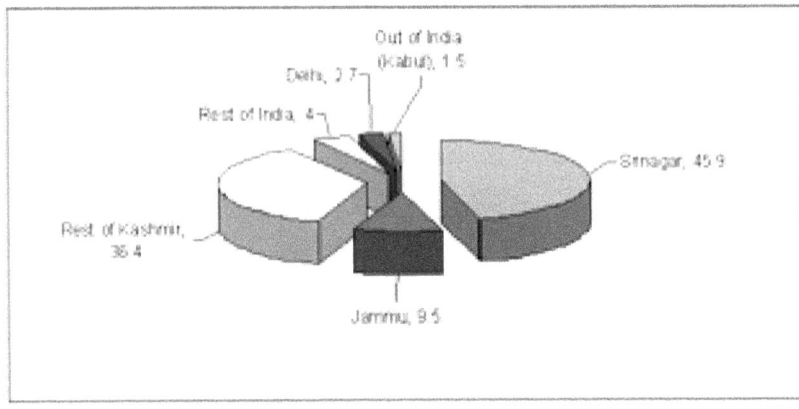

www.ingramcontent.com/pod-product-compliance
Lightning Source LLC
Chambersburg PA
CBHW052038270326
41931CB00012B/2541